D1104648

Twayne's United States Authors Series

EDITOR OF THIS VOLUME

David J. Nordloh
Indiana University

George Sterling

TUSAS 377

George Sterling

GEORGE STERLING

By THOMAS E. BENEDIKTSSON

Montclair State College

TWAYNE PUBLISHERS

A DIVISION OF G. K. HALL & CO., BOSTON

Copyright © 1980 by G. K. Hall & Co.

Published in 1980 by Twayne Publishers,
A Division of G. K. Hall & Co.
All Rights Reserved

Printed on permanent/durable acid-free paper and bound
in the United States of America

First Printing

Frontispiece photo of George Sterling reproduced through
the courtesy of The Bancroft Library,
University of California, Berkeley

Library of Congress Cataloging in Publication Data

Benediktsson, Thomas E
George Sterling.

(Twayne's United States authors series; TUSAS 377)
Bibliography: p. 173–76
Includes index.
1. Sterling, George, 1869–1926.
2. Poets, American—20th century—Biography.
PS3537.T42Z63   811'.52 [B]   79–28140
ISBN 0–8057–7313–4

Contents

About the Author

Thomas E. Benediktsson is an assistant professor of English at Montclair State College in New Jersey. Born in Cobleskill, New York, he attended Trinity University in San Antonio, Texas, and the University of Washington, where he received a Ph.D. in 1974. He has worked as a professional radio announcer and, before moving to New Jersey, taught at the University of Puget Sound in Tacoma, Washington. He now lives in Glen Ridge, New Jersey, with his wife and young son. *George Sterling* is his first book.

Preface

"What ever may have been the literary scene in America between the beginning of the century and the year 1914, it remains in my mind a complete blank. . . . The question was still: where do we go from Swinburne? and the answer appeared to be, nowhere."

Eliot's remark is prototypic of a dominant critical attitude toward the American poetry which preceded the First World War. There is justice in his statement: until Pound showed the way, there was no clear alternative to the subjectivism and rhetorical excesses of the Victorian tradition in which poetry was entrenched. But some of the implications of the statement (and of the attitude which underlies it) are not so just. Because the period between 1890 and 1915 is widely considered a "twilight interval," relatively little is known about it; it seems to be the minds of many students of poetry, a blank. It seems to be assumed that American poetry died with Whitman and Dickinson and was reborn with Frost. The great American poets of the twentieth century, seen in the immediate cultural context, seem to have sprung full-blown from nowhere, or Phoenix-like from the ashes of the Genteel Tradition.

These assumptions, in my view, create a distortion. The poetic rebellion of 1915 and the decade following is really the culmination of a mood of rebellion and experimentation which had been growing in the American intellectual world for years. To be sure, the official culture of the United States between the "Mauve Decade" and the First World War seems to be a monolith of genteelism, but an examination of the full range of intellectual and artistic endeavor proves that this period is as richly complex as any similar span in our history.

Even in poetry, shadowed in the "twilight" as it was, there were many who were trying to break free from the "envelope of the derivative" that muffled them, and to give new expression to an art which had succumbed to the vague idealism and trite sentimentality that perfumed the sanctioned pages of the *Atlantic* and the *Century*. The penalty for attempting the rebellion, of course, was public neglect and isolation, as the career of Edwin Arlington Robinson so vividly dramatizes.

This study of George Sterling will investigate the literary achievement of another such poet, a figure who in some ways was caught in the Swinburnean trap, but who in other important ways prefigured the change in sensibility which generated modernism in American poetry. Arthur Lovejoy remarks that in minor writers we can best understand the "tendencies of an age." In Sterling's work, the work of a poet who seems both behind and in advance of his times, we catch a glimpse of the remarkable ambivalence of turn-of-the-century America.

My thanks to Malcolm Griffith, who read this study in its earlier incarnation as a biography of George Sterling, and to Norma Long, who assisted in the preparation of the manuscript. To my wife, Lynn, whose constant encouragement and perceptive critical eye helped me through many months, I owe more than I can express here.

Thomas E. Benediktsson

Montclair State College

Chronology

1918 Carrie Sterling commits suicide.
1919 *Lilith: A Dramatic Poem.*
1920 *Rosamund: A Dramatic Poem.*
1923 *Truth. Selected Poems.*
1924 Meets Robinson Jeffers.
1926 Commits suicide in Bohemian Club, San Francisco.
1928 *Sonnets to Craig.*
1939 *After Sunset.*

CHAPTER 1

Biography, 1869-1905

ℂℂ THE urge to become a poet," George Sterling once remarked, "came to me at the scandalously mature age of
twenty-six."[1] The statement is true, but there had been present
in Sterling's character from the beginning a restless energy and
a disarming sort of rebelliousness which placed him at odds
with the rather stuffy norms of the bourgeois world into which
he was born. These impulses, which in that era might have
generated a capitalist like his uncle Frank Havens or a political
reformer like his friend Upton Sinclair, created a Bohemian and
a lyric poet.

I Revolt from the Village

During the second half of the nineteenth century, Sag Harbor,
New York, was a town of less than 4,000. Situated on Shelter
Island Sound, near the tip of Long Island, Sag Harbor had
achieved an independent economic existence through the pursuit of the sperm whale. By 1830 it was the second-largest
whaling port in the United States, and although the depreda-
tions of the confederate cruiser *Shenandoah* and the growing
use of kerosene brought the boom to its close, the whaling
influence remained strong in Sag Harbor through the years.
After the Civil War it settled into the calmer rhythms of a small,
decent coastal village. Whaling had made the town wealthy,
and the sober habits of its citizens helped make it a citadel of
upper-middle-class respectability, symbolized by the 200-foot
steeple of the First Presbyterian Church. The Old Whalers'
Church, as it was called, had served as a landmark for seamen
returning home. Then, and until it was blown down by a 1938
hurricane, the high steeple was the town's pride, representing

11

the dual heritage of its great whaling industry and the earnest Protestant discipline of its whalers. The Genteel Tradition dominated the ethos of this town, and it is therefore appropriate that George Ansel Sterling III, the "King of Bohemia," should claim it as his birthplace.

He was born on December 1, 1869, into one of the community's leading families. His mother's ancestors had lived in the Shelter Island Sound area since 1698, and his maternal grandfather, Wickham Havens, was one of the last of the great American whaling captains. Sag Harbor's past had its greatest impact on the child in the person of this patriarch, who had spent three decades at sea, first before the mast, finally as captain. Retiring to become a custom-house official and banker, Wickham Havens was a highly respected man in the community, as staunch a representative of Puritan virtues as Sag Harbor could produce. Sterling wrote of him admiringly that "he could cast the harpoon farther than anyone in the combined whaling fleets. As boyhood memory recalls him, he was built along the lines of an upright piano."[2] Wickham Havens and his whaling became the subjects of several poems, in which the central idea is much the same: the grandfather is symbolic of a masculine strength and a Yankee capability that are lacking in the poet and in general are lost to the world. These poems are evidence of an often overlooked aspect of Sterling's temperament; at times he felt that the raptures he learned to affect as a poet were inferior to the straightforward mastery of men and elements which his grandfather possessed unfeigningly.

If Wickham Havens became a sort of ideal for his grandson, it seems clear that the boy never really liked his father. George Ansel Sterling, Jr., a descendant of William Sterling, who had settled in Haverhill, Massachusetts, in 1662,[3] was the son of an Episcopal divine. Although a deeply religious man, he had renounced a possible calling to the ministry in favor of the medical profession. Having somehow avoided service in the Union Army, he was graduated at the age of twenty-two from the Bellevue Medical College in February of 1865. Shortly thereafter he settled in Sag Harbor, where he became an eminently successful physician with a large practice among both the permanent residents and the wealthy summer visitors to the

Hamptons. He married Mary Parker Havens in 1867, and George was the first of nine children, three boys and six girls. In some respects Dr. Sterling was a weak man. He drank heavily and surrendered to his wife a major share of his responsibility as a parent. He was unable to command the respect of his oldest son, and it is probably significant that George Sterling mentioned his father in print only once.

Mary Havens Sterling, on the other hand, was strong and dignified. She had inherited a good measure of her father's forcefulness, and for the Sterling children she was probably the dominant parent. She was a stately, decorous woman, physically very attractive, as were all of her children. Those who knew her in later life were impressed by her formality and careful attention to the proprieties of speech and manners.

On the surface, at least, George Sterling's first years were normal and happy. He was to look back on his childhood with nostalgia, describing the countryside that surrounded Sag Harbor as a "boy's paradise."[4] There was a shallow bay which warmed easily, offering fine swimming in the summers; there were woods with abundant wildlife and ponds which offered skating in the winter. He was given to the usual pursuits: swimming, fishing, pulling copper nails (worth 12 cents a pound) from old wrecks, picking huckleberries. He was remembered by boyhood friends as a cheerful youth, very alert to nature, who possessed the largest collection of birds' eggs in the town.[5]

As a child he showed only slight indications of an affinity for literature, and no indications whatever of precosity or genius. Before he first entered the Union Academy at Sag Harbor, his mother had taught him to read and write. His teacher, the Reverend J. J. Harrison, was later to remark that young Sterling was "one of the best scholars in English composition in his class,"[6] but this cannot be considered a sign of his vocation as a poet. More important as an impulse toward literature was the influence of Sterling's friend Roosevelt Johnson. Johnson's father, another doctor, had one of the finest private libraries in the state. Sterling used the library often; friends recalled later that he was an omnivorous reader, and "when engrossed in a book, it took a sharp call or a poke to divert his attention."[7]

In school Sterling received the usual training in the required subjects of the time; as he moved into the higher grades and was allowed to take electives, he studied marine biology, natural history, classical mythology, and astronomy. His informal education, however, was at least as important as the classes he took. Old sailors told him the names of spar lines and gave him basic instruction in navigation. Inquisitive and energetic, Sterling spent hours in his father's well-equipped observatory, "where he spotted the great comet of the eighties before the notices appeared in the New York dailies."[8] It was probably here that he first located the stars whose names—Altair, Aldebaran, Fomalhaut—were to find their way into many of his poems.

It is not certain when the boyhood idyll began to pall, but there are good grounds for speculating that Sterling's happiness was always threatened by tensions within his family. The atmosphere in his home must have become somewhat oppressive as his father's drinking increased with the years. In fact, several who have written about Sterling have commented that there was a strain of emotional instability among the Sterling men, manifest in George Sterling's alcoholism and his brother Wickham's addiction to laudanum.[9] The trait is apparent also, according to these commentators, in Dr. Sterling's two excesses: alcohol and Christianity. Of course great religious fervor is not in itself symptomatic of emotional instability, but it is very likely that some of Sterling's later bitterness about religion stems from a reaction against the enthusiasms—and the pressures—of his home.

During the early 1880s, religious tensions between the Sterlings and the community increased. The doctor was an Episcopalian with very traditionalist leanings; his wife's family, like most of Sag Harbor's elite, were Presbyterian true blue, and very hostile toward the excesses of either Methodism or Roman Catholicism. Most Sag Harborites, therefore, looked askance at Dr. Sterling's interest in the Catholic Church. And undoubtedly Mary Sterling's family was likewise disturbed by the zeal with which she herself adopted her husband's convictions.

As Sterling grew older, he became less able to abide the stuffiness of the town and the overpious atmosphere of home. Sag Harbor, so rich in possibilities for a small boy, offered little excitement to a youth entering his teens, and Sterling was unusually restless. His revolt was at first a rather vague striking out at authority, but it soon entered a more public phase, and it is clear that by his early teens he had discovered what would be a lifelong pastime: *épater le bourgeois.* Sterling and Roosevelt Johnson were the ringleaders of a gang of youths called the "Night Hawks," who were responsible for such gaffs as uprooting all the bathhouses and pushing them into the bay, each with its own signal light, and exhuming the amputated leg of a town official to carry it through the streets. According to an old acquaintance, "Whenever the town was Eulenspiegled— which was not too seldom—none of the knowing ones ever thought of going beyond these two serene young saints."[10]

The churches were frequent targets of the "Night Hawks." One midsummer Sunday evening the boys let loose 200 June bugs in the Episcopal Church; in the winter, they stuffed a wet gunnysack into the chimney of the African Methodist Church, whose weeping members were forced to evacuate. A particular incident stands out however, largely because in later life Sterling was so proud of the adventure.

When Sterling was perhaps sixteen, he and Johnson prevailed upon some of their sisters to conspire in a fairly elaborate prank. The girls stitched a pirate flag, which the following Sunday morning was discovered by a shocked and angered population flying from the peak of the 200-foot steeple of the Old Whaler's Church.

It had been no small feat. The boys had been forced to work at night, climbing a stairway to the base of the steeple and chinning themselves successively up the wooden ornaments which had been nailed there fifty years before. It is not surprising, then, that the skull-and-crossbones remained on the spire for a week, while the town's respectable citizens angrily sought the identity of the culprits. Sterling himself innocently offered to take the flag down for ten dollars, but ultimately a steeplejack was hired to perform the task.[11]

If the town had been scandalized by the pirate flag, it was shocked when shortly later one of its leading families converted to Catholicism. Dr. Sterling had been reading John Henry Newman and attending discussion groups of the Catholic Church; now he left his post as senior warden of the Episcopal Church and persuaded his family to embrace Catholicism. The Sterlings proselytized zealously for their new faith, and some say the shame was so great that Mary Sterling's mother, a staunch Presbyterian, felt constrained to leave town. Caught up in his family's enthusiasm, George Sterling agreed to begin a course of study preparatory to the priesthood. His rebellion, limited and harmless as it was, ended temporarily with his departure for St. Charles College, Ellicott City, Maryland, and it is only hindsight that can identify these outbreakings with the creative gift that was to remain dormant for ten more years.

At St. Charles College, then one of the few preparatory seminaries in the United States, Sterling was a good but not a brilliant student; surprisingly, he earned a good grade in conduct, indicating a sobriety far beyond what could be expected from a leader of the "Night Hawks."[12] He was not popular. In fact, some of his classmates later recalled him as a priggish youth, Northern-aristocratic, High-Church to his very eyelids.[13] Another, more sympathetic former classmate, characterized him as quiet, little given to the sports which formed the backbone of the school's leisure life, fond instead of walks in the woods, where he would display a surprisingly broad knowledge of birds and other small wildlife.[14]

There is no need to go to great lengths to explain Sterling's quiet conduct at St. Charles. He felt out of place there—and he was not the sort to rebel alone. When he first came to the school he had probably reconciled himself to the notion of becoming a priest; at bottom, however, he had no strong religious convictions, and the mobility which had made it easy for him to make the transition from Episcopal to Roman Catholic training soon made him realize that the structured existence at St. Charles was alien to his nature. Lacking coconspirators with whom to rebel, he was willing to conform; but, like Huckleberry Finn trying to pray, his heart wasn't in it. Not that he was unhappy—he had simply found no kindred spirits among the students and little inspiration from the faculty, with one notable exception: his teacher of English literature, the poet-priest John Banister Tabb.

Like Sterling, Tabb was an Episcopalian-turned-Catholic; unlike his pupil, he was fiery and passionate, as clearly a product of the antebellum South as George was of the Northern establishment.[15] Born in 1845, Tabb was the privately educated son of a wealthy Virginia family. Prevented by weak eyes from enlisting in the army, he became a successful courier for the Confederacy until June 1864, when his ship fell into Union hands. From that time until the end of the war, Tabb was a prisoner at Point Lookout, Maryland, where he met Sydney Lanier. Upon his release, Tabb taught school and prepared for the Episcopal ministry, converting instead to Catholicism in 1872. Ordained a priest in 1884, he taught at St. Charles for the next twenty years, publishing meanwhile several volumes of poetry and a large body of magazine verse.

Father Tabb was a very popular and effective teacher; he succeeded in instilling a love of literature in the most prosaic and earthbound of his students. That he did so with Sterling cannot be doubted. Old schoolmates remember Tabb stopping George on the playground, giving him lines of Keats or Shelley to memorize before he went back to his recreation.[16] But although Tabb found Sterling a willing and intelligent pupil, it is questionable that he recognized in him a latent poetic gift. Still, in years to follow Sterling often referred to Tabb's example as his first true literary impulse. In Sterling's first book of poems, *The Testimony of the Suns*, appear the lines "On Reading the Poems of Father Tabb":

> So airy sweet the fragile song,
> I deemed his visions true,
> And roamed Edenic vales along,
> Lit by celestial dew.
>
> Illusive gleamed the timeless bow'rs;
> The winds and streams were such
> As Eve had mourned—but ah, the flow'rs!
> Too delicate for touch![17]

The poem attempts to be both an acknowledgment of Tabb's literary influence and a critique of the naive Christianity with which Sterling felt Tabb's poetry was suffused. Tabb's literary influence could not have been very strong or immediate, however, because until 1896 Sterling's ignorance of poetics and of the principles of composition was great. Furthermore, Tabb's

lyrics were short and compressed, more like Herrick's or even
Emily Dickinson's than like the stately Swinburnean lines and
loose poetic structures of Sterling's poetry (the poem above is
not a representative example).

Aside from giving him his personal friendship and introducing
him to English poetry, Tabb performed one other great service
for Sterling. Toward the end of Sterling's stay at St. Charles,
Tabb told him categorically that he had no vocation for the
priesthood, and he advised him to seek another profession. It
is likely that Tabb's advice helped him to defy his parents'
wishes when, in the summer of 1889, he decided not to return
to St. Charles for further religious training.

During these St. Charles years, George Sterling had spent
his summers in Sag Harbor, the months passing in the same
carefree way as those of his boyhood. As before, Sterling and
Roosevelt Johnson swam and picked huckleberries, though now
they regaled themselves with cigars and stolen brandy as well,
and no doubt occasionally found time for *épater le bourgeois*.
The summer before Sterling's last year at St. Charles—he was
then eighteen—a new acquaintance came to Sag Harbor. This
was the famous welterweight Pete McCoy, who, renouncing the
ring, had come to live with his brother-in-law. McCoy immediately attracted a cult of young admirers, but he rejected all but
Johnson and Sterling, who were able to win his comradeship
through gifts of cigars, beer, and bourbon stolen from Dr. Sterling's sideboard. A simple, cheerful man, he entered in all their
activities with relish, enjoying the adulation of Sterling and
Johnson more than the gifts they offered.

But after Sterling had returned to school that fall, Pete McCoy
went to Rhode Island for a small-purse bout with a younger
boxer. Not as durable as he had been in his prime, he was
battered to his knees by a fighter who would have been an easy
victim two years earlier. Bitterly disgraced, McCoy threw himself over the rail of the steamer that was taking him back to
Sag Harbor. Many years later Sterling wrote of Pete McCoy:

. . . to what protracted death-struggle—he, a good swimmer—who
shall say? And who may tell what other source of despair and
bitterness gave rise to such an action? He who had faced his hun-

dreds of opponents in bloody and protracted fights, year after year, when pugilism was a sterner matter than now, went down before the onset of this last adversary. We were to see Pete no more, nor ever again to sit thrilled by his pantherish skill: his bones mossed with the small weed of the tidal waters, these thirty-six years.[18]

In some ways, Sterling's summer friendship with McCoy was a trivial incident in his life; yet it involves some important elements of his character—the worship of masculinity which strongly affected his relationships with both sexes; the desire to be associated with a prestigious person, later manifest in the ways in which he ingratiated himself with famous literary men; and, finally, the obsession with suicide which was so tragically woven into his later experience.

More immediately, Sterling's refusal to return to St. Charles created grave family difficulties. His mother was very disappointed by his rejection of the priesthood, and his father was disturbed by his lack of motivation to enter any profession whatever. Furthermore, the household had become cramped in the past few years; the Sterling children now numbered nine, only three of whom—the boys, George, Wickham, and James—had gone away to school. George's return added new tensions to an already crowded and high-strung atmosphere.

The elder Sterlings, determined to make something of their son, returned to their earlier plan of preparing him for the medical profession. But clearly he had as little vocation for medicine as he had had for the priesthood. He was bright but willful and immature, little disposed to accept further pressure from his parents, who must have seemed intent on pushing him in unwanted directions—more for their own motives than for any real desire to meet his needs. Furthermore, Sag Harbor was becoming more unpleasant daily. The town which once was a "boy's paradise" had become a kind of purgatory, and Sterling must have felt contemptuous of those narrow-minded ones who now predicted a bad end for all the young degenerates. Roosevelt Johnson had been arrested and fined for "malicious mischief,"[19] and Sterling, though not in legal trouble, was exploring the waterfront dives in search of any new experiences Sag Harbor could offer.

As might be expected, Sterling's relationship with his father, never very warm, was worsening. The doctor's practice had expanded considerably of late, until at this time or shortly after he was forced to maintain dual residences in Sag Harbor and New York City. His drinking increased correspondingly, and the stomach ulcers that plagued him so much later had appeared. George, too, had begun drinking enthusiastically if not heavily, already developing his fatal weakness for the "white logic" of alcohol.

It was not long before matters reached a climax. When Sterling announced officially to his father that he was sure that he would not become a doctor, Dr. Sterling decided to support him no longer. He accused his son, justly, of lack of ambition and said that he should leave Sag Harbor to "go West and be a businessman."[20] Sterling's uncle, Frank C. Havens, who had left Sag Harbor under similar circumstances many years before, now was a wealthy Oakland realtor. Havens agreed to employ his nephew, and in 1890 George Sterling left for California, entirely unaware of the shape of his future there. According to a widely repeated story, Sterling chalked a piece of doggerel on the station platform shortly before his train was to depart:

> Sag Harbor, now I'm leaving you;
> I bid you now farewell.
> Whene'er I hear you spoken of
> I'll surely think of Hell.[21]

It might have been his first poem.

II   *Threshold*

When he stepped off the train in Oakland and, truly, for the next few years, Sterling's life was poised among alternatives. Foremost now, of course, was the possibility of becoming a businessman in the footsteps of his uncle, who had left Sag Harbor under similar circumstances some twenty-seven years earlier. Havens was president of the Home Benefit Life Association, a company which was soon to give way successively to his American Investment Union and ultimately to the Realty

Syndicate, which he organized in 1895 in partnership with Francis Marion (Borax) Smith.[22] The Realty Syndicate would dominate real estate and public utilities in the Oakland area for several years, and Havens would become a millionaire.

On the eve of this expansion Sterling had been offered a position as a clerk, with possibilities for rapid advancement. He lived at his uncle's home for some time and remained diligent and restrained. Lacking the catalytic agency of a personality stronger than his own, he stuck to his newly disciplined life until the next year, when his friend Roosevelt Johnson came to Oakland. It was Johnson who urged him to meet the first literary figure who would have a lasting influence in his life—Joaquin Miller.

Back in Sag Harbor, Johnson and Sterling had been entranced by the grandiose rhythms of Miller's *Songs of the Sierras*. They were fascinated by the exploits of this frontiersman who had made a "literary pilgrimage" to England in 1870, and had caused a sensation among the London social elite. Praised by Rossetti and Swinburne, who felt that they had discovered in him another Whitman, Miller had returned to California an internationally known poet. After some years he settled into the life of a picturesque local sage—resplendent in chaps, sombrero, and shoulder-length hair, and attracting scores of visitors who came to "the Hights [sic]," his wooded estate above Oakland, to chuckle at his eccentricities or to be shocked by his morals.

During the summer and fall of 1891, Sterling and Johnson made a regular journey up the thousand-foot hillside to "the Hights." Often they would find the patriarch fully clothed in bed, with long yellow hair streaming out from under a red skullcap, while his disciples labored at the stone monuments to Fremont, Browning, and Moses. It was the weekly gathering place of a group of young artists and poets, and so it was that Miller introduced Sterling to part of the circle that would nurture his muse.

Miller enjoyed being the center of attention, and his guests in turn were delighted by the old man's eccentricities. Sterling especially enjoyed the elaborate hoaxes that Miller would stage for female visitors, like the "Modoc rain-chant," which was climaxed by a shower on the cabin roof, created by the turning of a hidden faucet. Taken with this type of exhibitionism, Sterling began some posturing of his own. Roosevelt Johnson recalled an occasion that year when the two staged a bitter quarrel and a mock duel with shotguns for Miller's amusement. Unfortunately, they miscalculated the safe distance and actually peppered each other with birdshot.[23] On another occasion, Miller told Sterling that he looked "like a fool." Sterling responded that he was afraid that he looked like a poet.[24] Already he was conscious of the profile which would elicit from the press the *ad nauseam* comparisons with Dante. And it is interesting that Sterling was conscious of looking "like a poet" long before the ambition to write poems actually struck him.

It is clear, then, that Joaquin Miller was a strong formative influence on Sterling's development as a poet—but not through his poetry. True, there is a certain grandiose quality in the poems of both men—Sterling's nature poems and Miller's extravagant paeans to California scenery display a similar exuberance—but not because of Miller's influence. Miller's flamboyant rejection of middle-class values gave Sterling a lasting impression of how a poet should *act*. Sterling was all his life preoccupied with being a poet, and there is no doubt that his posturing in later years can be traced to this grand *poseur*, who compensated for his lack of talent with incessant role-playing. But it was not until the next year that Sterling met the man who was to have the greatest influence on his work—Ambrose Bierce.

Although Sterling had not read Bierce's *Tales of Soldiers and Civilians* until he came to California, he had heard much since then about this great critic and author who also wrote acerbic columns for various California newspapers. At this time Bierce was enjoying a reputation as the "Rhadamanthus of West Coast letters," passing judgment on the poetry of the day and serving as literary tutor to several aspiring poets. Sterling was delighted when, in 1892, he was invited by Albert Bierce, the brother of Ambrose, to spend a few days at Albert's camp on Lake Temescal, near Oakland. He was even more pleased to find that Ambrose Bierce would also be there. Then twenty-three, Sterling was so overwhelmed at meeting Bierce that when the older man, prevented by his asthma from using a tent, slept by the fire, he bedded down near him. Not used to sleeping on the ground, Sterling awoke frequently. He wrote later, "Whenever I did so, I saw Bierce lying with his face to the sky, the deep blue eyes staring up at the fainter blue of the star Lyra."[25]

Flattered by Sterling's naive hero-worship, Bierce was also impressed by the young man's quick mind. Although his asthma soon drove him away from the Lake Temescal camp, he thought well enough of Sterling to invite him to lunch at Marchand's in San Francisco. There Sterling was too awed to reply as Bierce pronounced one of his *obiter dicta*: "My boy, the only important thing is to think clearly."[26] Bierce was amused at having to explain the point of a risqué joke to Sterling, but he enjoyed the adulation, and soon the two were walking or dining together frequently.

Bierce and Miller were two survivors of a fascinating period in the literary history of the American West—San Francisco's original Bohemia. Several young writers, dislodged and scattered by the Civil War, came to California in the 1860s. Drawn by the gold fields, they remained to pursue literary careers; Mark Twain, Ina Coolbrith, Bret Harte, Bierce, and Miller were among the writers who gained national prominence during the 1870s. Then with the popularity of the *Overland Monthly* and the *Golden Era*, American literary Bohemianism acquired a new stereotype.[27] Corresponding to the European version of Bohemianism—starving elegantly in a garret, or writing strange hallucinatory sonnets in the brothel where one's tubercular Mimi danced—was a new, home-grown American version, a frontier Bohemia, where one squatted by the campfire and discussed Rossetti and Morris over a meal of canned beans. Whitman, of course, had been the precursor, and by the mid-1890s Bliss Carman and Richard Hovey made a poetic industry of "Vagabondia." By establishing friendships with Miller and Bierce, Sterling himself was unknowingly preparing to make his own unique contribution to American Bohemianism. And when after Havens's marriage he moved to the famous Montgomery Block, a San Francisco building which housed the studios of many artists,[28] Sterling established even stronger ties with the Bohemian community.

Thus, in the first two years of his residence in California, Sterling had established the fulcrum on which his life would balance for some time. Evenings and weekends he was the embryonic poet and latent Bohemian. During the weeks he was the earnest young businessman, favored protégé of Frank Havens the financier. The conflicts between these two styles of life were not yet uncomfortable—until his marriage.

Sterling's promise as a businessman, along with his cheerful, energetic nature and sensitive, finely molded features, made him one of the most eligible men in either of his circles. It is certain that his private secretary found him so. She was Caroline Rand, sister of Lila Rand Havens. Both Carrie and Lila were "high-colored, Junoesque" women who had been among the first wave of women in business. They were the daughters of a New Hampshire policeman, David H. Rand, and they were both ambitious. Lila had realized her ambitions by marrying her employer in 1892; Carrie saw a similar opportunity in George Sterling. She was a lovely girl; Sterling was attracted to her; doubtless his uncle and aunt encouraged him; and they were married on February 7, 1896.

The honeymoon, however, was traumatic. Both of the Sterlings were miserably seasick en route to Hawaii, and during the honeymoon Sterling lost twenty-two pounds. Refusing to see any of the tourist attractions, he sulked in their hotel room and wrote his first serious poem, a blank-verse narrative which is no longer extant.[29] After this disastrous episode, the Sterlings rented a cottage in the lower Piedmont hills above Oakland. On the surface, at least, they made the necessary adjustments and were happy together.

They had been married for six months when Dr. George Sterling and the rest of the family moved from Sag Harbor to Oakland. Failing health and alcoholism had forced the doctor to interrupt his practice the year before. Now he had decided to go to Hawaii to run a plantation. But when the family reached Oakland, it was obvious that Sterling senior was in no condition to continue; he died five months later, on March 8, 1897, fifty-four years old.

It was at some time between his marriage and his father's death that Sterling decided to become a poet. The past five years in California had been important in the chain of experiences and influences that led to his decision. His contacts with literary

Bohemia (most notably embodied in Joaquin Miller) had provided him with a model of the artistic personality—flamboyant,
histrionic—that he found irresistable. His excessive admiration
for Ambrose Bierce had led him to accept the critic's belief in
the supremacy of poetic genius over any of the other talents of
men. The younger literary men that Sterling had met in Oakland and in San Francisco's Montgomery Block had played a
part. And finally, his need to break free of the conventional
pattern that his new wife and his uncle's business sought to
imprint upon him prompted his rebellion into poetry.

When, in 1897, Sterling sent his first manuscripts to Ambrose
Bierce for comments, he began one of the most important relationships of his life. This, the strangest apprenticeship in American literary history, would last nearly ten years.

III *King of Bohemia*

Chapter 3 will discuss Bierce's literary influence on Sterling
and the development of what Jack London called a "cunning
and deep philosophy of life,... worked out on a basis of disappointment and disillusion."[30] But while Sterling was earning
his laurels under Bierce's tutelage, there were other influences
that drew him away from absolute allegiance to his mentor,
and also away from his comfortable life with Carrie Sterling.
By 1900, he was still the young executive, but as he passed
thirty and remained only Havens's personal secretary, it became
increasingly evident to his family that he would not become a
captain of commerce. This generated tensions, as did the increasing influence of Socialist thinking and Sterling's growing
local fame as a poet and a Bohemian.

Sterling first came directly in contact with socialism through
friends. Blanche Partington, member of the multi-talented Partington family of San Francisco, and Austin Lewis, an English
lawyer who had organized some of the first Socialist Labor party
chapters in the western United States, were probably the first
sincere Socialists in Sterling's acquaintance. Sterling frequently
attended meetings of the Ruskin Club in Oakland, and several
members, including Frederick Irons Bamford and Herman Whitaker, became his close friends. Noxious to Bierce and inimical

to the capitalist ideology of his family, socialism appealed nonetheless to a generous side of his nature. He felt for the poor a
sympathy and a responsibility which sprang from a natural
humanitarian instinct. His personal bias against materialism
developed into a conviction of the widespread misuse of wealth,
the subject of many poems:

> Grown soft,
> Thy hands reach out for mercenary joys;
> Thy heart desires dishonorable loves
> And baser dreams. . . . Now the land
> Grows vile, and all thy statehood is a mart. . . .[31]

But ironically enough, while Sterling was writing Socialist
poems like the above, he was helping his uncle create a business
empire.

Several other contradictions affected Sterling's socialism. Many
of his letters and poems indicate that he felt superior to and
set apart from the masses, so much so that he could not believe
wholeheartedly in the equality of all men. But more important,
the characteristic "cosmic" perspective that he was learning to
develop as Bierce's disciple made it impossible for him to believe in the perfectibility of human society. If all of man's efforts
to improve his condition are ultimately and equally doomed,
socialism is as false and vain a doctrine as Christianity. Sterling
was able to practice a sort of mental legerdemain which made it
possible for him to profess socialism sincerely and to support
his Socialist friends vigorously, but it is clear that his ultimate
allegiances were to his ideal of art rather than to humanity.

Accordingly, it was as a Bohemian and a poet rather than as
a Socialist that Sterling began to make a name for himself in the
San Francisco area. His association with Bierce was a guarantee
of a certain degree of local renown. Beyond this he had begun
to publish verse frequently in periodicals in the area, and his
home in Piedmont was becoming a center for Oakland-based
writers and artists. Before long Piedmont would contain a
thriving artists' colony, and by 1904 Sterling would be known
as "King of Bohemia" in San Francisco, a title he wore with
pride for most of the rest of his life.

Sterling had of course become a member of Oakland literary and artistic society before his marriage in 1896. Toward the turn of the century he assumed a more central social role as the group would spend afternoons in the Piedmont hills and evenings at the Sterling home. By 1901 Oakland had a recognizable Bohemian colony. Aside from Sterling and his grown-up sisters, there were Dick and Blanche Partington, Albert and Carleton Bierce (the latter the nephew of Ambrose), Austin Lewis, Herman Whitaker, the young sculptor Robert Aitken, and newspapermen Joseph Noel and Will Irwin.[32] Although they often called on him for a shot of whiskey and a tall tale, Joaquin Miller was no longer a central figure. His direct influence on Sterling had declined because of Bierce's harsh criticism of his poetry, and for the most part Miller remained on the periphery of the Piedmont group, now dominated by the artist Xavier Martinez and by Sterling himself.

Martinez had studied in Paris, and injected a strong measure of Latin Quarter style into the group, with his long black hair, baggy corduroy trousers, and flowing red ties. But if Martinez brought a European sophistication, Sterling made a contribution of his own. Will Irwin wrote later, "I never saw a man who took more delight in life than the young Sterling. Ranging the Piedmont hills to witness the blaze of poppies and the luminous shadows of live oaks, playing some childish game of scrub baseball, noting the beauty of a woman, spouting favorite passages in Shelley or Shakespeare; laughing at a joke—whatever he found to enjoy, struck him with a kind of rapture."[33] Others who remembered the Piedmont outings concurred, suggesting that there was in Sterling a natural and innocent impulse to pleasure, and that it was in the outdoors that he was most himself. At this time, despite his attempts to juggle several different styles of life, Sterling seems to have been able to put aside the contradictions and obey the impulse to live completely in the present and be the eternal boy. In retrospect, there is something almost Arcadian about these Piedmont Bohemians. They were not yet disaffected; they had rebelled against their elders, but their rebellion took the form only of harmless diversions, like bloomers and cigarettes for the women, liquor and ballgames for the men. *Épater le bourgeois* was a sport, not a means of preserving a precarious sense of identity. As yet there was no sense of the straining to remain avant-garde, no hint of the alienation that would over-come so many of them; as yet, there were no suicides.

In fact, at the time the only casualty was George Sterling's career as a real estate baron. Carrie had by now come to realize that the numerous properties in Sterling's name were only blinds to keep the public from knowing the extent of Havens's interests. When the connected transportation system of the Alameda County railroads and the Oakland–San Francisco ferry was being built by Havens, Sterling transferred the waterfront prop-erties in his name to his uncle. Carrie Sterling was disturbed by this revelation, and she was further dismayed when Sterling was not promoted on several occasions. Havens's interests now included banks and newspapers, and Carrie had hoped that Sterling could have been installed as assistant manager or assis-tant editor of one of these. But Sterling was not interested; he was content to draw his salary as a glorified secretary and to try to keep business as far as possible from his real sphere of concerns. But the true crisis in his domestic life did not begin until he became bosom friends with another young writer, one who was not content merely to pose as a Bohemian; he was Jack London, and Sterling met him in the spring of 1901.

As rising young writers in the Bay area, both London and Sterling had heard of each other before they actually met. It took some time, however, for the two to be comfortable to-gether; London was drawn neither to Sterling's aristocratic leanings nor to his bourgeois sensibilities. Until he proved him-self an unqualified success as a writer, London was tormented by an excessively acute sense of his own origins—his illegitimate birth, his lack of formal education, his memory of a very recent period during which he starved himself to afford stamps and envelopes for manuscripts.[34] A few slumming trips to the Bar-bary Coast and to Chinatown, however, soon convinced London that Sterling was a boon companion.

After he moved to the Piedmont district in 1902, London read "The Testimony of the Suns" in manuscript and became con-vinced that Sterling possessed a great poetic genius, far superior to his own talents as a mere storyteller. Furthermore, he began to believe that Sterling was a true aristocrat, not a bourgeois pretender to culture. Both men were largely self-educated, but at this time Sterling was better read than London in the materialist philosophy that they both espoused. Sterling was noted among his friends as a prodigious talker, and London's respect for his mind grew after long hours of conversation, usually over a bottle. "Probably better than anyone else with whom Jack was acquainted, George understood what he meant by the 'white logic' of John Barleycorn."[35]

Evidence of this respect is plentiful, but the best indication of London's feelings about Sterling at this time is his portrayal of "Russ Brissenden," a character modeled after Sterling, in his autobiographical novel *Martin Eden*. Brissenden initially strikes Eden as "anemic and feather-brained."[36] Upon subsequent meetings Eden realizes that he actively dislikes the man. However, when Brissenden and Eden have a drink and a long conversation, suddenly Eden discovers what sort of mind he is dealing with. Brissenden is a genius; he combines a poet's beauty of language with a philosopher's wisdom: "[His] thin lips shaped . . . mellow phrases of glow and glory, of haunting beauty, reverberant of the mystery and inscrutableness of life."[37]

Brissenden becomes a sort of spiritual advisor to Eden, admonishing him not to worry about the magazines but to "love Beauty for its own sake." He teaches the unsophisticated young writer to enjoy the refinements of food and cherish wines. Brissenden is a hedonist, possessed by a madness to live, to thrill, "'to squirm my little space in the cosmic dust whence I came,' as he phrased it. . . ."[38] The portrait moves closer to the facts of Sterling's life when the enigmatic Brissenden disappears mysteriously for two weeks, returning with a long poem entitled "Ephemera," which from its description is "The Testimony of the Suns." Eden is staggered by its artistry, and even after Brissenden's suicide and his own rise to fame, he still believes that "Ephemera" is "infinitely greater than anything he had ever done."[39] It is the disillusionment with a public that fails to reward truly superior minds like Brissenden's that sends Eden to his own death. Aside from its fascinating anticipation of both their suicides, *Martin Eden* is a testament of London's high regard for Sterling's intellectual and poetic achievements.

For London, Sterling became his "Man-Comrade," the great

friend for whom he had longed since he was a boy. In fact, it was probably the youthful quality in Sterling that he most admired—the eternal boy, filled with merriment. And like all boys, before long the two had given each other nicknames: Sterling was "'the Greek"; London, "the Wolf." The nicknames were perfectly appropriate to the poses that the men affected. Sterling was "the Greek" because of his profile, and because of his "paganism." London was appropriate as "the Wolf" because of his primitivism. He would later complain to his second wife that she did not call him "Wolf" enough; and when he built his ranch in the Valley of the Moon he named his house the Wolf House.[40] Likewise, Sterling cherished the image of himself as a pagan demigod somehow transplanted to California. Sterling's aristocratic poses and his basic dignity of manner did not conflict with London's horseplay; consequently they did not have to worry about stealing scenes from each other.

In those pre-Freudian days, the two men had no compunctions about declaring their fervent love for each other. They would have been shocked and disgusted had anyone suggested that they had latent homosexual feelings.[41] And yet there is no doubt that Sterling and London found in each other in these years a warmth and rapport that neither found in another human being, male or female. The lives of both men are similar in the respect that neither of them had a completely satisfactory relationship with a woman. London always sought women who would fit one of his abstract definitions of "Womanhood" or who would meet the needs of his ego; Sterling became a classic version of the Don Juan, attracted to many women sexually and seeking emotional transcendence in stylized, "poetic" affairs, but unable to retain a constant relationship with any woman, including his wife.

After London entered the Piedmont group, he quickly became its central figure. The picnics and gatherings began to adapt to his boisterousness. Rough pranks and horseplay became more common, and people drank more heavily. It was apparent to most that London did not truly fit into this group of genteel rebels, that there were pressures within him that did not allow him to relax into this dilettante's world. Beneath his public image he was tormented by his past, and there was always a tension in him between his hatred of the bourgeoisie and his desire to enter and dominate it. Before long the vapid gestures of rebellion of these Bohemians had begun to bore him. Sterling's personal compromise, too, had become onerous and confining.

In 1903 the literary careers of both men were on the rise, but both were unhappy with their personal lives. With a wife, a home, and two small children, London began to realize that the life he had planned had failed to quench his restlessness. The disillusionment that may then have been a pose for Sterling became a harsh truth for London, and the two spent many nights away from home, carousing in the city. Carrie Sterling played the role of the neglected wife, moving out of the bedroom after one of Sterling's debauches. Sterling's mother began to believe that London was responsible for this, and embarked on an unsuccessful campaign to counteract his influence. But she was wrong; London only acted as a catalyst to allow Sterling to follow his own inclinations. After London divorced his wife and left the Piedmont group (as rapidly as he had entered it), Sterling continued to spend most of his time in the city, enjoying his new celebrity.

With the publication of *The Testimony of the Suns and Other Poems* (1903), San Franciscans became aware of the "new poet of Keatsian promise" in their midst. Symbolic of Sterling's new fame was the invitation to join as a non–dues-paying member the most exclusive men's club in the city, called, ironically enough, the Bohemian Club. He also began to frequent Coppa's, a Montgomery Block restaurant which was a gathering place for a group of writers, artists, and journalists who were so proud of their Bohemianism that they painted murals of themselves on the walls. Sterling's picture was accompanied by two of the most grotesque lines from the yet-unpublished "A Wine of Wizardry": "The blue-eyed vampire, sated at her feast,/Smiles bloodily against the leprous moon."[42] Coppa's was a perfect illustration of the paradox of Bohemianism, a social rebellion that looks for applause to the society it condemns.

Sterling thrilled with pride when newspaperman Idwal Jones dubbed him "King of Bohemia," and undoubtedly he was glad to use his reputation as one of the city's most elite young writers

to help form liaisons with women who found the combination
of his personal charm and his local fame hard to resist. In fact,
Gelett Burgess remembered Sterling from the Coppan period
as "a lean, temperamental, eager girlhound, hunting with Lafler
[another young Coppan] in couples."[43]

For several years now, Sterling had been conducting an incessant series of casual affairs; these were to continue without inter-
ruption until his death in 1926. Dissatisfaction with his marriage
may have been either a cause or an effect. Years later he wrote
with some bitterness to a friend, "When I think of my own
youth, sex starved until I came to California at 20 (and then
no one but prostitutes for years) I could put in a fortnight
swearing."[44]

Like his poems, Sterling's love affairs were attempts to experience transcendent raptures through extremes of sensation.
Hence their briefness. When London and Sterling discussed sex,
they often would rationalize their escapades with the "law of
ascendant mating." This was one of London's favorite ideas, that
a woman will naturally—even biologically—prefer a tenth share
in the affections of a man of genius to the total love of an ordinary man. Sterling believed also that sex was a way of releasing
the subconscious creative impulse: Mary Austin later remarked
that he "was always ridden by restless impotencies of energy
which only by sharp exaggeration of sensation would find their
natural outlet in creative expression,"[45] the main catalysts being
alcohol and sex.

Most of Sterling's friends were aware of his peccadilloes and
tried their best to withhold knowledge of them from his wife.
But in 1904 Carrie Sterling heard that her husband had been
meeting women in a Montgomery Block room rented expressly
for assignations.[46] The rumor was true, and it led to the first real
crisis in Sterling's marriage. Carrie had become reconciled to
Sterling's failure in real estate, but she could not accept his
heavy drinking and his neglect of her since he had become so
celebrated as a Bohemian.

It may have been this first marital crisis which led to their
decision to leave the San Francisco area and move to a "farm."
Increasingly Sterling had been resentful of his obligations to
Havens: they interfered with the time he had for composition,

and he felt that the routine of clerical work was inimical to the spirit of a Bohemian poet. Secretly bored with the Coppa ritual as well, Sterling was eager to sample another type of Bohemianism—an unencumbered wilderness life far from the distractions of the city. Carrie believed that he might be able to control his drinking and his "poetic affairs" in the absence of temptations. Both of them were enthusiastic when they heard of the cheap land at Carmel-by-the-Sea, a beautiful village to the south of Monterey.

But this move to Carmel would be no retreat from "cities wrung by care/ Awhile in ancient solitudes to sink."[47] Founding the Carmel colony would gain for Sterling a national fame as a Bohemian poet, further conflicts among art, socialism, and economic survival, and ultimately would lead to an American literary tragedy.

CHAPTER 2

Biography, 1905-1926

I *Carmel*

THE seven years George Sterling spent as founder and "high panjandrum" of the literary colony at Carmel were pivotal ones in his life. During this time he achieved a national reputation both as a poet and as the leader of one of the nation's most important Bohemian groups. He acquired many new friends, including Sinclair Lewis and Upton Sinclair, and played an important role in their lives. Conversely, he broke with Bierce, lost some of his intimacy with London, saw the failure of his marriage, and learned some of his limitations as a poet and a human being.

The history of the Carmel colony during the same span reflects important forces in the cultural history of the United States. As it moved beyond its first phase as Sterling's own particular Walden, and beyond the period shortly after the earthquake when it served as a place of temporary refuge for San Francisco's homeless artists, Carmel became part of a burgeoning national phenomenon. In New England, in the Midwest—even in Florida —groups of young intellectuals who shared unconventional views were leaving the cities to create cooperative living groups in a rural setting. This proliferation of colonies can be seen as part of the mood of experimentation and escape that was characteristic of the prewar period in America, and the evolution of these groups, especially of Carmel, shows a pattern of increasing alienation that eventually culminated in the postwar "Lost Generation."

As we have seen, Sterling's interest in Carmel sprang from his disillusionment with his job and with the distracting Bohemian life of San Francisco. A major impetus to settle there,

34

however, came about as a result of his meeting with the novelist Mary Austin in late 1903, when the two decided that a community of professional writers could be established there. By the summer of 1905, Sterling was ready. Financed by the ever-generous Havens, he bought a lot and built a house in a pine grove a half-mile from the townsite of Carmel-by-the-Sea. In October the low bungalow, dominated by a long room with a huge square fireplace, was finished.[1]

Sterling's initial idea of his life at Carmel was Waldenesque: "Well, you see why I must raise vegetables, Belgian Hares, hens and the fruit of their wombs, squabs and gold fish, 'keep a bee,' raid mussel-reefs, and cultivate a taste for rice—not to mention cold water and 'just one girl.' I'm determined to get into black and white unnumbered multitudes of lines that ramp up and down my innards, eight a-breast."[2] He had rented three acres in front of the house for cultivation, and hoped to live an active, simple life of gardening and poetic creation. His enthusiasm was such that he began to sound like an "uplift" speaker: "Our best happiness—almost our only one—has always come from the sense of well-being that accompanies a good digestion and a clean liver, which are possible to both of us only by the simplest sort of living (diet), accompanied by long hours of sleep."[3]

And yet Sterling does not seem to have been totally honest with himself. At the same time that he was extolling the virtues of a solitary life, he was writing glowing letters about Carmel to all of his friends, and he had designed a living room with entertaining clearly in mind. There had been plenty of company all summer, and already the regime of "cold water and 'just one girl' " was becoming difficult. And as far as work was concerned, his entire poetic output for the year was the hastily composed *The Triumph of Bohemia*, a verse-drama written for the Bohemian Club.

Coppan Arnold Genthe built a cottage in Carmel that fall, and Mary Austin arrived in January of 1906. Now well established, the Sterlings saw the fruition of their dream of a simple life. Visitors were numerous, and mussel bakes or hikes to the beach were frequent occurrences. To most of those present, Sterling seemed the embodiment of the spirit of the place. Just as he had been at his best in Piedmont on the picnics, here the

atmosphere brought out his most charming qualities. Mary
Austin recalled that "Sterling's greatest pleasures were those that
whetted his incessant appetite for sensation—the sting of the surf
against his body, the dangerous pull of the undertow off the
Carmel beaches, or gathering seafood among the undulant,
apple-green hollows of the Mission Cove."[4] All in all, Carmel
was proving to be a perfect rural atmosphere for the pursuit of
the Muse—except that Sterling was not writing anything. But
this first, peaceful phase of the Carmel colony came to an abrupt
end on April 18, 1906.

The Sterling diary for that day reads, "Earthquake knocked
over chimneys—Monterey isolated—breakdown of telegraph and
telephone. Began 5:15 A.M—lasted 15 sec."[5] In the next two days
much of San Francisco was destroyed by fire. The catastrophe
did not, however, come as a savage personal blow to Sterling.
Most of the second edition of his *Testimony of the Suns* was
destroyed when Robertson's warehouse burned, but he had lost
no friends or relatives. Coppa's had been destroyed, and those
who ate a last memorial dinner in the ruins were convinced
that San Francisco's Bohemia had perished in the fire. But it
was soon established that Bohemia was very much alive 100
miles to the south in Carmel. And from relative isolation in
March, by the end of May Carmel had become a haven for
many of the Coppans and most of the Piedmont group.

The situation had a natural effect of putting off, once again,
Sterling's plans for work. He had been talking for months of a
verse drama that he would write about Lilith, the legendary
witch, subject of poems by Mackenzie and Dante Gabriel Rossetti. As the social obligations of the summer increased, he put
off work on the play. In late July he wrote to Jack London that
he wanted to write *Lilith* and "get it off my mind."[6] But the play
would not be completed for ten years, and Sterling's total output
for the summer amounted to a few sonnets and a blank-verse
piece which was clearly of little value.

In November 1906, Jack London came to Carmel for the first
time. His arrival was the beginning of a five-day party which
featured the inevitable beach picnic, long discussions in the
Sterling living room, and an excursion down the coast. During
the picnic, Genthe noted and later recorded a memorable scene:

George Sterling, who was proud of his classic contours, had climbed to the top of the cliff in his bathing trunks. Somewhere or other he had procured a trident and he was standing silhouetted against the sky while Jimmy Hopper was taking his picture. This was too frivolous for Mary (dressed in the beaded leather costume and long braids of a Indian princess) who was gazing at the setting sun. Standing on the beach with outspread arms, she began something which sounded like an incantation, but which turned out to be a quotation from Browning: "Tis a Cyclopean blacksmith," chanted Mary, "striking frenzied sparks from the anvil of the horizon!"

London was standing with a fork in hand, having just disposed of an abalone steak. Taking a look around which included both Mary and the horizon, he exclaimed, "Hell! I say this sunset has guts!"[7]

The perpetual beach picnics were the central feature of Carmel's social life during this period. Some of the work problem had been solved by a general agreement that no writer was to be disturbed before noon. The morning's work completed, the rest of the day was devoted to diversion. If tides were low, Sterling, Hopper, and others of the more adventurous would pry abalone from the rocks. *The Abalone Song*, created by Sterling but with verses contributed by many others, became a stock feature of the folklore of Californian Bohemia. While the group were pounding shellfish to tenderize them, they would sing in chorus verses likes these:

> Oh! Some folks boast of quail on toast
> Because they think it's tony
> But I'm content to owe my rent
> And live on Abalone.
>
> Some live on hope, and some on dope,
> And some on alimony;
> But my tom cat, he lives on fat
> And tender abalone.[8]

Sterling and Mary Austin set the tone for these celebrations. Both loved to act out their fantasies, and both had a sense of what would generate the greatest impact. Sterling nailed up in a glen a circle of cow skulls as a "pagan altar"; Mary Austin wrote in a tree-house on her property, which she called the

"Wickiup." The two seem to have had a sort of rapport; they found that their fantasies were complementary, and Mary Austin's novel *Outland* was based upon a piece of make-believe that she and Sterling had worked out together in Carmel.[9] She later remarked that "there might even on a time have been a faun type of man whose psychological make-up would have been something like George's imperfectly humanized, having the intellects and will of man, but emotions and instincts almost wholly of the wild creature sort, incapable of abandoning the one or being entirely faithful to the other."[10]

Her description was compatible with the romantic image of himself that Sterling chose to project. Despite earlier resolutions to make Carmel a solitary retreat, he was now eager to help promote it as a new Bohemia and, simultaneously, to enjoy the attentions of an admiring public. Sterling was not delighted, however, when in September 1907 *Cosmopolitan* published "A Wine of Wizardry." Suddenly Sterling and Carmel were famous or, rather, notorious.

After two years of unsuccessful attempts to place "A Wine of Wizardry" in various periodicals, Ambrose Bierce had turned to his own *Cosmopolitan*. The publication of the poem was offered as a counter to a recent remark made by the British ambassador to the United States that America had no poets. A foreword to the poem stated that it alone was "proof that there is at least one poet in America."[11] In the same issue Bierce supplied an article entitled "A Poet and His Poem," in which he praised Sterling immodestly: "I steadfastly believe and heartily affirm that George Sterling is a very great poet—incomparably, the greatest that we have on this side of the Atlantic. And of this particular poem, I hold that not in a lifetime, has our literature had any new thing of equal length containing so much poetry and so little else. . . . It has all the imagination of 'Comus' and all the fancy of 'The Faerie Queene.' If Leigh Hunt should return to earth to part and catalogue these two precious qualities he would find them in so confusing abundance and so inextricably interlaced that he would fly in despair from the impossible task."[12]

The outcry, of course, was enormous. A storm of protest arose on both sides of the Atlantic over Bierce's excessive praise.

Ignoring its actual merits, critics complained about the poem's grotesqueness, its lack of religious sentiment, its lack of unity, its lack of restraint. They were most of all outraged that Bierce should rate the unknown Sterling so high on Parnassus. Bierce retaliated with a satiric article, "An Insurrection of the Peasantry," published in *Cosmopolitan* in December 1907. Bierce defended himself with a broadly ironic attack: "Naturally, not all protagonists of the commonplace who have uttered their minds about this matter are entitled to notice. The Baseball Reporter, who says Mr. Brisbane, 'like Mr. Sterling, is a poet,' the sweet singer of slang, the Simian Lexicographer of Misinformation, and the Queen of Platitudinasia who has renounced the sin-and-sugar of youth for the milk-and-morality of age must try to forgive me if I leave them grinning through their respective horse-collars to a not unkind inattention."[13] Bierce did point out eloquently the inhibited and limited tastes responsible for part of the outcry. However, to those familiar with Sterling's role in helping Bierce finance the publication of *Shapes of Clay*, the charge of "log-rolling" was very hard to refute.

As a result of all this publicity, Sterling's relatively quiet life in Carmel was now interrupted by large numbers of curious visitors who wanted to see the Bohemian poet, and who stole chips of wood from his chopping-block for souvenirs. He received hate mail from outraged readers of the *Cosmopolitan*—and a fairly substantial amount of praise as well. He became convinced that the publication of the poem had been merely a publicity stunt of William Randolph Hearst, and wrote bitterly to London, "It's as though he had launched a drove of swine into my big sitting room, or had dumped a can of sea-sick vomit on my head."[14] The furor had barely subsided when another sensational item reached the press. On November 13, the beautiful blonde poet Nora May French committed suicide with cyanide at Sterling's Carmel home.

Despite the fact that gossip immediately linked her with Sterling, the two were probably not romantically involved. She had been depressed and nearly suicidal on many recent occasions, and her death did not come as a great surprise to her friends. But the suicide created a tremendous furor in the press, and as months passed, her death began to assume nearly legendary proportions. Sterling himself became quite obsessed with her memory, and eventually wrote many poems about her, of which the following sonnet, written in 1908, is fairly representative:

> I saw the shaken stars of midnight stir,
>   And winds that sought the morning bore to me
>   The thunder where the legions of the sea
> Are shattered on her stormy sepulcher,
> And pondering on bitter things that were,
>   On cruelties the mindless Fates decree,
>   I felt some shadow of her mystery—
> The loneliness and mystery of her.
>
> The waves that break on undiscovered strands,
>   The winds that die on seas that bear no sail,
>   Stars that the deaf, eternal skies annul,
> Were not so lonely as was she. Our hands
>   We reach to thee for time—without avail,
>   O spirit mighty and inscrutable![15]

And significantly, it was not long after Nora May French's death that the Carmel group began to talk obsessively, "almost voluptuously," about suicide as the only appropriate death for a poet or a hedonist.[16] Eventually her death became the impetus for what nearly could be called a cult. When Carleton Bierce, who worked for the mint, came to visit, Sterling and others asked him to obtain some cyanide for them. They divided the poison into small vials for each person, with the pledge to use it when the time came that life was too painful or too meaningless. Both Carrie Sterling and George Sterling would choose this "poetic" way of death.

The fall of 1907 had been a very important season for several reasons. First, the publication of "A Wine of Wizardry" had signaled Sterling's emergence into national recognition as a poet. Furthermore, his dependency on Bierce's critical judgments had declined; the years to come would see him moving farther from the older man's influence and from his regard. Finally, Sterling had become nationally famous as a Bohemian poet at the same time that Nora May French's death had portended the more serious alienation that was to characterize American Bohemianism in the years to come.

In June 1908 Sterling received the sanction of the literary establishment when Richard Watson Gilder of the *Century* accepted his "Three Sonnets on Oblivion." The sonnet was a very effective vehicle for Sterling, and he was becoming known as a master of metrical variations within the limitations of the form. But for the most part his muse was idle during 1908, as it had been since the move to Carmel. His wife, Carrie, who had hoped that Sterling would be able to write verse that would "sell," grew nearly desperate as the months passed. The town was full of new people, most of whom, drawn by the newspaper coverage of Sterling's "paradise," were the wealthy pretenders and university professors who comprise the usual camp-followers of Bohemia. Sterling, who took a naive delight in adulation, seemed content to play the public poet's role for these people, as he had been earlier at Coppa's. There were several young female compensations for his lack of poetic production that summer; secretly, however, he was bored, and when Upton Sinclair wrote expressing an interest in Carmel, Sterling wasted no time in urging him to come.

Troubled by a series of domestic problems and chronic indigestion stemming from overwork, the author of *The Jungle* rented Arnold Genthe's cottage for the winter. Sinclair settled down immediately for a season of hard work and regained health. Health was easily acquired, but time to work was not, and Sinclair fell prey to the renowned Carmel lethargy. Sterling, on the other hand, was spurred by the presence of Sinclair into his most productive period since the move to Carmel. But Sinclair's real influence on Sterling can be measured by the following incident.

In late November Sinclair was featured at a Ruskin Club meeting, and Sterling had agreed to give the introduction. But unfortunately Sterling spent the afternoon drinking with friends, and by the meeting time he was too drunk to read the Socialist poem he had written for the occasion. Sinclair, an avid Prohibitionist, was hurt and shocked: "This was the first time I had ever seen a great mind distorted by alcohol."[17] He informed Sterling the next day that he would leave Carmel. But swearing to stay on the wagon as long as Sinclair remained in Carmel, Sterling persuaded him to stay.

Surprisingly, he kept his pledge. After Sinclair left Carmel that spring, Sterling continued his program of moderation for several months. They were to remain friends for many years, in spite of the most discouraging forces imaginable—including Sterling's love-affair with the woman who became Sinclair's second wife. It seems clear that Sinclair, despite the intensity about moral issues which led Sterling to brand him a "zealot," had a strong influence on Sterling. He was the first to introduce Sterling to health and diet fads which became a lifelong preoccupation; he was the first writer to lead him to question the value of drinking; and for a time he inspired him to take his socialism more seriously.

By the time Sinclair left to rejoin his wife, several other writers from the East had come to Carmel. Among them were Michael Williams, Grace MacGowan Cooke, and a young man from Yale named Harry Sinclair Lewis, who was shortly joined by his classmate William Rose Benet. When Lewis left Carmel, Sterling was able to find a position for him on the staff of the *San Francisco Bulletin*; thus Sinclair Lewis joined the growing list of younger writers whom Sterling had been able to help.[18]

But for Sterling, still the center of Carmel's social life, the distance between him and these eager, talented young men must have become troubling. He was now forty, and his hair was gray. He began to assume a defensive, self-deprecating tone about his age at the same time that he was acting more the youth than ever. Despite this, he was happy with his respected position in Carmel; as Lewis wrote of him many years later, "I am most touched by remembering him as the King of Carmel, living serenely (at least apparently) with Carrie, looking over his cup of jade from his front porch, sitting with all us brats by his splendid fire of pitch-pine."[19] Carmel seemed perfectly suited to him; as he wrote to Bierce, "Well, in the meanwhile I exist, and am rather happier than I deserve to be. . . . There's a certain deep satisfaction in merely *existing*, here."[20]

A Wine of Wizardry and Other Poems appeared in 1909. As a collection of Sterling's best work since the publication of *The Testimony of the Suns and Other Poems* in 1903, it left something to be desired in the matter of length. Aside from the title poem the book contained only thirty-five poems, most of them sonnets. Many of those, however, demonstrated the maturing of Sterling's talents; though he was not writing as much, his work was improving. His name was now well established, and his sonnets were finding their way into the best eastern periodicals. With their publication came admiring letters from several poets, and Sterling began thinking of making a trip to the East to make contacts with the New York literary world. But before he could make concrete plans, his mentor Bierce announced that he would visit California for the first time in eleven years.

In 1907 Bierce had been as enthusiastic about Carmel as had Sterling; however, as his former pupil began to show signs of moving from his sphere of influence, he had become more skeptical: "I'd not *live* there and be 'identified' with it, as the newspapers would say. I'm warned by Hawthorne and Brook Farm."[21] Accordingly, when Bierce visited Carmel, he stayed at a hotel nearby, refusing the rustic comforts of the Sterling home. He seemed to be losing his respect for Sterling. On one occasion, when they were boating on the Russian River, Sterling was wearing a brief pair of bathing trunks. Bierce told him harshly to dress himself appropriately before they met his niece, a few hundred yards downstream. By the end of this visit, Sterling must have realized how much his relationship with Bierce had changed. The older man had become increasingly intolerant and accusative; and Sterling himself, now no longer in need of literary help, had lost most of his earlier submissive manner.

London also had changed. When he returned from his Pacific cruise, London and Sterling celebrated together as of yore, but it seemed to his friends that London had become more egocentric than ever, and he drank more. He had yielded to a growing physical lethargy which was beginning to undermine his health, and he seemed to be more interested in adding acreage to his ranch than in writing good books.

Both Bierce and London seemed disillusioned and misanthropic when Sterling saw them in 1910, and it is noticeable that his own attitudes picked up a definite touch of cynicism. He was more open about his extramarital affairs than ever before;

he asked London to market short stories for him under London's own name;[22] and he had become increasingly misanthropic; "Human beings make me think of a rock-rolling episode of my early days. One of the rocks went farther than we dreamed it could, and smashed the knee of a cow's foreleg. The other cows promptly began to gore her."[23] In early 1911, when Van Wyck Brooks came to Carmel for a few months, he noticed that Sterling "had precisely the aspect of Dante in hell." He was not impressed with the atmosphere of Carmel: "They [the Carmel writers from the East] gave themselves over to daydreams while their minds ran down like clocks. . . . For this Arcadia lay, one felt, outside the world in which thought evolves and which came to seem insubstantial in the bland sunny air."[24]

Sterling, however, had conquered his own lethargy. The four-year poetic drought that he had suffered was over, as demonstrated by the appearance in April 1911 of *The House of Orchids and Other Poems*. It received a very favorable series of reviews in the eastern literary press, and June 1911 found the Sterlings in Sag Harbor—the first visit Sterling had made to his birthplace in twenty years. In New York City that fall, Sterling met Mary Craig Kimbrough, a beautiful young novelist from Mississippi. In a grand romantic gesture, he wrote her a sonnet a day for 100 days.[25] She later married Upton Sinclair, and the sonnets were published after Sterling's death in *Sonnets to Craig* (1927).

After their return to Carmel, the Sterlings separated. More cynical than ever, drinking more heavily, and indulging more openly in an incessant series of affairs, Sterling had worn out his wife's patience. They were reunited briefly in the summer of 1913, but the September death of Sterling's brother Wickham and the November disappearance of Ambrose Bierce may have spurred Sterling into more excesses. In December Carrie Sterling filed for divorce on the grounds that her husband drank heavily and would not support her.

The trip to New York had made Sterling aware that his poetry, though fairly well known and admired by the more conservative literary critics, was quite old-fashioned to younger writers. Yet in 1912 Harriet Monroe asked him for some poems, which appeared in the third issue of *Poetry*, and his "Ode on the Centenary of the Birth of Robert Browning" won a second prize

in the *Lyric Year* contest which many literary historians have
regarded as a harbinger of the new poetry. After the divorce
settlement, Sterling decided to assail in earnest the eastern literary marketplace, and he began to make plans for another trip
to New York—this time, perhaps, forever.

II *The War Years*

Bierce's impending break with Sterling had been obvious ever
since his visit to California in 1910. Sterling had moved too far
from his sphere of influence, and Bierce was never able to maintain a friendship unless it was strongly tinged with *noblesse
oblige.* To put it most generously, we could say that despite
his cynicism Bierce had two standards of human value, both of
them eminently personal—a standard of art and a standard of
conduct. Sterling met his standard of art but failed miserably
in the other category. One's affairs should be discreet; but Sterling's love-sonnets, written in triplicate and sent to any woman
who caught his fancy, hardly met a criterion of discretion. Furthermore, Sterling's Bohemian poses were disgusting to Bierce,
who was offended by the tales of such escapades as "diving
drunk as a fiddler's bitch into a park pool at midnight, of appearing at a fancy-dress ball indecently draped in a leopard
skin, of playing the crazy fool generally."[26]
Sterling's insistence on adhering to the pernicious doctrines
of socialism was especially abrasive. As one of his later comments to Sterling would imply, Bierce's hatred of radical politics
approached fascism: "What this country needs—what every
country needs, occasionally—is a good hard bloody war to revive
the vice of patriotism on which its existence as a nation depends.
Meantime, you socialers, anarchists and other sentimentaliters
and futilitarians will find the civil-service your best recruiting
grounds, for it is the Land of Reasonless Discontent. I yearn for
the strong-handed Dictator who will swat you all on the mouth
o'you till you are 'heard to cease.' "[27]
To these general objections to Sterling's behavior, Bierce
added some imagined personal affronts. For example, Sterling
had been unable to afford the $100 price of Bierce's *Collected
Works*—a leather-bound accumulation of nearly every word

Bierce ever published, from his fine Civil War stories to the most insignificant of newspaper squibs. As a consequence Bierce felt insulted and neglected that his friend would fail to subscribe to his twelve-volume bid for fame. Sterling finally subscribed in 1912, but not before Bierce had discovered new causes for resentment.

In fact, Bierce had grown rancorous and critical of all his friends, and it was clear that his bitterness had approached a pathological condition. In his last visit to California, he remarked to his niece Lora that soon he would go to Mexico, from which he never planned to return—"and nobody will ever find my bones."[28] He made similar remarks to many friends, and most of his biographers conclude that Bierce went to Mexico to die: "To be a Gringo in Mexico—ah, that is euthanasia."[29]

Before he crossed the border Bierce wrote bitter and vindictive letters to many of his remaining friends. His letter to Sterling was typical. Addressing him as "Great Poet and Damned Scoundrel," Bierce maintained that Sterling had taken $600 from him in 1903, when he was supposedly financing *Shapes of Clay*. He charged Sterling further with an act of character assassination which led to the breaking of Bierce's engagement with a lovely California woman.[30] Both charges were false and deeply hurt Sterling, who had been Bierce's loyal friend for twenty years.

Many months passed before Sterling became convinced that Bierce had died in Mexico. Characteristically, he held no personal rancor for the way he had been treated by the man he had admired so deeply. In later years he would reevaluate the effect that Bierce's counsel had had on his poetry and would write without regret that "although he has been accused of laying a hand of ice on my muse, I can testify that he gave of his counsel generously and with acumen. . . . In view of the modern movement in poetry, he was not, perhaps, the best master I could have known, but I cannot look back to the days of my apprenticeship without feelings of gratitude."[31] And when Sterling finally conceded that Bierce must have gone to Mexico to die, he wrote a eulogy that casts the best possible light on Bierce's motive:

> Be sure his purpose was a pride,
> A matter not of fear but taste.
> When finding mire upon the waste
> and hating filth, he turned aside.[32]

It may well have been that last unjust letter from Bierce in November 1913 that prompted Sterling to go on the binge which caused Carrie to leave him for the last time. When the interlocutory divorce decree was issued in January 1914, Sterling made no protest. He gave his wife all that he owned except for a few books and paintings. He was now eager to go to New York: "I'm getting nervous living in this graveyard of emotions and hotbed of memories."[33] He was determined to remain on the wagon, and he believed that he could make a living as a writer of salable stories and poems if he could get "the disease of art" out of his system.[34] After he assembled the materials for his fourth book, *Beyond the Breakers and Other Poems*, Sterling wasted no time in preparing for his journey.

April 15 found Sterling in New York, where he joined Upton Sinclair in picketing the Standard Oil Building in protest against the burning of a camp of striking miners in Colorado. By June 15 he had moved to Sag Harbor, planning to spend the summer at work on poems and short stories. Using the unlimited credit of his name there, he moved into a hotel room and began the regime which had brought success to London: a thousand words of prose—or one complete poem—each morning. He was a total abstainer now (or so he told his correspondents), and he was determined to crack the New York literary market. Perhaps because one completed sonnet was easier for him to compose than a thousand words of hated prose, his efforts produced a series of thirty-five sonnets on the war in Europe. These and five short-story manuscripts were the product of three months' work, easily his most productive period in years.

Perhaps it was their very facility which affected the quality of his work. There was no market for the sonnets; Sterling was able to place only a few poems in periodicals; and the short stories failed to arouse any interest at all, even though he now had a literary agent, Paul Reynolds, who was trying industriously to find publishers. Sterling was forced to remain in Sag

Harbor far longer than he had anticipated. The stack of stories grew from five to ten, and his credit remained good, but he was unable to leave until he had some income.

By October he had become very restless. He complained to Albert Bender about the editors: "They turn down my best and even my most human work and take stuff from obscurer writers that is far worse than mine."[35] And yet, he continued, all the poets that he had met in New York were familiar with his work, and most had praised it. It seemed ironic, he went on, that he who needed so little should be denied even a mere living. His letter was really a plea for help, and Bender, a patron of dozens of needy California artists, responded as generously as always: he immediately wired Sterling the money he needed to move to New York.

By Christmas Sterling was well in debt to Bender, and he had grown so threadbare that Mary Sinclair had more than once slipped a quarter into his suitcase as he departed from a visit. Aside from a few poems and an occasional short story, he had been unable to market his work. Discouraged, nearly defeated, he began to feel a kinship with the bums who froze in Times Square while the more affluent warmed themselves in the bars. He knew that only the bounty of a few friends separated him from them. He would bring tramps to his room now and give them scrambled eggs, whereas only a few years ago he had objected to London's treatment of his experience as a hobo, remarking that tramps always reminded him of "an evil smell."[36]

In the middle of a dreary, despairing January, Sterling received help from an unexpected source: The *San Francisco Examiner* commissioned him to write an ode for the Panama-Pacific International Exposition. They would pay him 50 cents per line, and five days of vigorous rhyming produced 257 lines of poetry and a substantial sum on the horizon. This windfall was enough to make him certain that he could return to California in the spring.

With his acceptance of the commission to write an ode for the Exposition and his decision to return to California, Sterling accepted, at least temporarily, his failure to make a name for himself in New York, and settled for a role as civic poet in

San Francisco. He had tried to write for the marketplace, but had found that his standards of art made him as unsuitable for Washington Square as he would have been for Grub Street. In returning to California he was not accepting a role as literary regionalist; though his standards were as universalized as ever, he was compensating for his lack of popular appeal by becoming an occasional poet.

Upon his return to San Francisco, Sterling was amused to read the lines of poetry carved into the architrave of the Exposition and inscribed SHAKESPEARE, MILTON, STERLING. The juxtaposition, reminiscent of the old Coppa's, had been transformed from a spoof designed to shock the more respectable citizens into an effort to boost local "culture." Sterling had been transformed along with it from a rebel against bourgeois decorum into a somewhat dilapidated civic institution. A year later, he was honestly flattered when the San Diego Exposition honored him with a "Sterling Day." But the real measure of his failure was the opinion of the newer poets, typified by Harriet Monroe's review in the March 1916 *Poetry*:

Now if I cannot quite rise to the Californian estimate, at least I can find in Mr. Sterling a gift, a poetic impulse, which might have carried him further than it has yet. His first long poem, "The Testimony of the Suns," does, indeed, make one feel the sidereal march, make one shiver before the immensity and shining glory of the universe—this in spite of the shameless rhetoric which often threatens to engulf the theme beyond redemption, and in spite of the whole second part, an unhappy afterthought. Already the young poet's brilliant but too tactile craftsmanship was tempted by the worst excesses of the Tennysonian tradition: he never *thinks*—he *deems*; he does not *ask,* but *crave*; he is *fain* for this and that; he deals in *emperies* and *auguries* and *antiphons*, in *casual throes* and *lethal voids*—in many other things of tinsel and fustian, the frippery of a bygone fashion.[37]

Although Sterling pretended indifference, the article hurt him deeply: "I got a neat little roast in the March number of 'Poetry.' The funny part is that the old girl is probably correct! Peace to her undemanded maidenhead!"[38]

In the fall of 1916, after the publication of *The Caged Eagle and*

Other Poems, Sterling was struggling to maintain his self-confidence in the face of overpraising locals and condescending younger poets, and financial circumstances that obliged him to write hack-work almost exclusively. It was during this time of personal uncertainty that he learned of the suicide of Jack London, forty-one years old.

London's mental and physical health had been deteriorating for some years, especially after 1912. In that year his "Wolf House" burned to the ground on the day of its completion, and he abandoned himself to uncontrolled eating and drinking. Attacks of uremia caused him severe pain, but he continued his diet of cocktails and undercooked duck. He became overweight and physically lethargic, and was subject to severe insomnia; soon he was taking morphine to ease the pain and to permit sleep.

Once, after a monumental binge in 1911, London had offered to form a suicide "compact" with Sterling: "When our work is done, our lifeforce spent, exit laughing. Is it a promise? We hereby agree not to sit up with the corpse."[39] On the night of November 21, 1916, London suffered an unendurable kidney calculus. He used a pad next to his bed to compute a lethal dose of morphine, and he died the next evening, never having regained consciousness.[40] Sterling was one of the few who knew the truth about London's suicide. His death certificate had officially listed the cause of death as uremic poisoning, and it would not be until 1938, when Irving Stone's *Sailor on Horseback* appeared, that the general public knew the actual circumstances.

Like those from Bierce, London's last words to Sterling were bitter and unjust. He had written him on October 28, reproaching him "for not having kept his promise to come up to the ranch, and citing all the inconvenience he had caused the servants by his failure to show up as scheduled."[41] Sterling helped supervise the cremation, wrote a titled memorial poem to be read at the funeral, and acted as coexecutor of the will. At the funeral he remarked flippantly to Charmian London that he would not give up "while there is sex in the world."[42] But there was now a great gap in Sterling's life: his beloved Wolf was dead.

After the shock of London's death Sterling plunged himself into activity, but with no particular success. When the theatrical producer Richard Ordynksi approached him to do a blank-verse translation of Von Hoffmansthal's *Everyman*, he immediately immersed himself in the project. Unfortunately, the play closed within a week of its opening in January 1917, and Sterling's hopes for a substantial income from royalties vanished. To add to his problems, years of drinking had begun to undermine his health, and he became subject to fits of depression. He wrote to Blanche Partington not long after London's death, "About the pleasure-pain proposition: I've no time to argue about it with pen and ink. It seems to me that pain is absolutely as much a reality as joy, and present at this stage of evolution in many more and intenser forms than joy. As Heine says, 'What interval of bliss was ever so protracted as many of those of pain?' "[43]

In this time of personal frustration and loss, the war in Europe provided a sort of outlet. As the probability of U.S. intervention in the war grew closer, Sterling became more ardent in his support of the Allied cause. Perhaps the war was an outlet for the personal frustrations and losses of recent years. Too old to enlist, Sterling exerted his energies in writing war verse and contributing to the propaganda effort. His hatred of the Germans became almost pathological as he yielded completely to war-hysteria. He wrote chanting, chauvinistic poems on the war; he was particularly proud of one with a Service-like, table-pounding rhythm and clichéd lyrics entitled "The Binding of the Beast," which appeared in *The Binding of the Beast and Other War Verse* (1917). Sterling openly admitted, however, that it was more propaganda than poetry:

Now frothing in his rage, a scourge to youth and age,
Caked with blood he stands at bay, with his feet upon his prey.
Ringed with surf of guns resounding, raw and fetid from the
hounding,
Smiles he still on baffled fury and the roar of hate release;
But the huntsmen of the ranks, with their steel at breast and
flanks,
Give no truce nor sign of respite at the binding of the Beast.[44]

At the end of the war Sterling wrote to Blanche Partington, "I'm sorry it ended with any Germans left alive. . . ."[45]

The war was cathartic for Sterling in several ways, and by its end he found that he had the time and inclination to return to a serious work that had remained unfinished for years. This was *Lilith*, which he completed in May of 1918. Encouraged by the project and finding himself a little ahead financially, he decided to brave the New York literary scene once again. In July he left for New York; upon arriving, he immediately made contacts with some of his friends from 1914, and met other writers for the first time, most notably Theodore Dreiser and Edna St. Vincent Millay. All was well: Macmillan made a flattering proposal to publish a selection of his poems; however, Sterling decided to "stick to Robertson," his San Francisco publisher. New York was exhilarating this year of the armistice, and in Upton Sinclair's words, Sterling was "revelling" in Greenwich Village when the word came from California that his ex-wife had killed herself.

After separating from Sterling, Carrie had gone to live with her sister, Lila Havens. For a while she was employed by Havens to take care of his private gallery of Oriental *objects d'art* and Russian paintings. But Havens's financial empire was crumbling, and soon he was unable to pay her a salary. Furthermore, she missed the social life of Carmel and the stimulating company of Sterling's friends. After Havens's death in May 1918, Carrie Sterling's depression grew deeper, and on August 7 she arranged her hair, put on a dressing gown, and on the phonograph beside her bed played Chopin's *Funeral March* as she took a capsule of cyanide.[46]

Sterling returned to California immediately: "It was an awful trip, listening day after day to what the car-wheels had to say about me."[47] He did not visit the hilltop in Piedmont where her ashes were strewn; he did return briefly to Carmel but could not stay:

> So like a ghost your fragrance lies
> On the path that once led home.[48]

He spoke little about her death, but wrote to Charmian London

on the twenty-fourth, "Yes, Charmian, let us both see it through:
I too have that fast hold on life, and am prey to illusion. I
know it's illusion; but it seems worthwhile even at that. It will
be time enough to open 'the outer gate' when one is old and
feeble."[49]

In the five-year period which coincided with the war in
Europe, the three persons closest to Sterling had died. Bierce
had sought the "enchanted forest" in the Mexican desert; London had found freedom from pain through an overdose of
morphine; and his former wife, failing to be "poetic" in life,
had tried to make her death a work of art. He himself had come
to realize that his physical health was deteriorating, and that
his poetry would never be widely read. In order to recover his
integrity in the years that remained him, he would have to come
to terms with these losses.

III   *Bohemian in Residence*

After his return from New York in 1918, Sterling moved to
the Bohemian Club, where an anonymous benefactor paid for
his room on "Poor Man's Row." He lived there until his death.
Journalist Idwal Jones recalled that "the room was plastered
with photographs and drawings, some, indeed pinned flat on
the ceiling so he could gaze at them when he awoke. Some were
of the stern, personable Bierce, a packet of whose letters he
invariably carried in his breast pocket; many were of himself,
in the attitudes of a boxer; in leopard-skin with sandals and
garland of flowers, his Nijinsky-like rainment at the artists' ball;
or nautical in jersey at the tiller of a boat."[50] Sterling was now
more self-consciously "Bohemian" in the 1920s than he had been
during the war. He was aware that many viewed him as a link
with the pre-earthquake era of the Coppans, and he was careful
to cultivate the role of a living symbol of San Francisco's
Bohemian past. He "scandalized several masked balls in San
Francisco" by appearing in a leopard skin or a toga, with a
laurel wreath on his brow. He "created an international sensation" with his midnight nude swims in the Golden Gate Park.
Although he was past fifty, he boxed often with professional
boxers. But he remained conscious always that these were only

attempts to evoke an era which had passed, a youth which had vanished.

And yet, since the publication of *Lilith*, Sterling had recovered his pride in his work. An indication of this is his quarrel with William Stanley Braithwaite of the *Boston Transcript*. He was irritated with Braithwaite over the misprinting of his poems and the excessively long time his submissions were kept. But more important, Braithwaite came to represent to Sterling the lingering sanctimoniousness of the genteel tradition: "After reading, as I just have, your last anthology, I am more than ever convinced that you are opaque to pure poetry, that you miss 'the soul and inner light of song,' and fail to note when the baser rock passes into crystal. You care for assertions, optimums and pieties, and become art-brother to that absurd old hunker [William Lyon] Phelps, whose breath of life is platitudes and sanctimonies."[51] At about the same time, he refused the invitation to join the American Institute of Arts and Letters, because, he remarked, "I discovered on its roster the names of Bob Chambers, the foremost literary whore of his day, Ned Townshend, once a purveyor of putrid slang, and the impossible Wm. Lyon Phelps, who left me out of his book on American poetry because he thinks me unholy!"[52]

Sterling began now to seek out the friendship of writers he respected, quite possibly to fill the gap left in his life by the deaths of London and Bierce. If there was one friend of the 1920s who might have taken the place of Bierce in his esteem, it was H. L. Mencken. Mencken's *Smart Set* and later his *American Mercury* frequently published Sterling's poems. The correspondence between Sterling and Mencken centered around Sterling's contributions to the magazines, but their relationship extended beyond the roles of editor and poet. To Mencken, Sterling was a true poet and a kindred spirit in his love of drink and women and his hatred of the genteel tradition. To Sterling, as I have hinted above, Mencken was an Olympian mind, an insightful social critic, and an avatar of the sensibility of Bierce. Like Bierce, Mencken was the foremost social critic of his times to attack the hypocrisies of the American bourgeoisie; also like Bierce, he was fond of romantic poetry. As he had done earlier with those of Bierce, Sterling began to carry

Mencken's letters in his breast pocket to read to his friends.

In 1920, after Prohibition had changed the pattern of San Francisco's nightlife, Sterling cast himself into the role of unofficial guide of visiting writers to the city's alcoholic underground. For example, when Mencken came in July of 1920 to cover the Democratic National Convention, he asked Sterling to provide him with a carouse in the Bohemian quarter, enough "grappo" to make him happy, and a female companion who was sturdy, because, as he said, "I am somewhat heavy, and it takes muscle to get me into bed when I am in liquor."[53] Sterling entertained Mencken with such success that the latter recommended the experience to Theodore Dreiser.

Sterling had met Dreiser during his New York visit of 1918. When a year later Dreiser moved to Los Angeles, Sterling wrote him, urging him to visit San Francisco where, he said, "the daughter of the vine, though shy, can still be found by the faithful. And there are other daughters."[54] Dreiser, who had already formed a favorable opinion of Sterling's poetry, was pleased by the invitation. In mid-October he came to San Francisco to attend a reception in his honor and to accept Sterling's offer of the best of the city's varied delights. Dreiser enjoyed himself hugely and wrote afterward to Mencken: "I have been up to S.F. and am locoed. I expect to move & spend my declining years there. . . . George Sterling hovers over it like a burnished black Holy Ghost. . . . Nightly I was led to my room full to the ears. Oh, happy land, oh shapely succubi."[55]

Two years later the novelist returned to San Francisco, this time in the company of Helen Richardson, who lived with Dreiser to the end of his life. Again Sterling and Dreiser talked for hours on end on all subjects, from the implications of infinity to the possibility of reform in America. One evening, passing through Golden Gate Park at three in the morning, they stopped to enjoy the beauty of a lily pond. Suddenly Sterling, exhibiting his well-known passion for nudity, undressed on the bank and swam gracefully to the center of the pond to gather water-lilies for Mrs. Richardson. She was appropriately captivated, writing later of his swim as a "water dance that Nijinsky or Shankar or Mei Lan-fang might have dreamed up."[56] A policeman accosted them, but when Sterling identified himself they were released—

an indication of the public tolerance of Sterling's escapades. The following morning both the *Chronicle* and the *Examiner* had the story, but only Dreiser and Sterling were identified. Sterling was so delighted by the publicity that he swam the lily-pond several times in the next two years—doing his best to keep Bohemia alive.

Sterling's attitude toward Dreiser was complex. On one hand he respected Dreiser as a major critic of American society and a standard-bearer against the false moralism of the "custodians of culture," who were then making a last-ditch stand in attempting to censor *The Genius*. However, he found him in person a little lumbering and obtuse, lacking the intuitive leaps of London or the precision of statement and epigram that he had admired in Bierce. Hence his witty but somewhat condescending nicknames for Dreiser: "Titanothere," "Megatherium," "Good Old Elephant."

If Sterling felt a little superior to Dreiser, it is certain that Dreiser admired Sterling very highly. When he read *Lilith* for the first time he wrote to Sterling of its merits: "Your Lilith is . . . a casket of rare similies—light on ice;—a lake of moods and sighs. Between 8 and 2 the other night I read it and thought of Shelley, Keats and our own Poe."[57] He became convinced that Sterling was "the ranking American poet, greater than any we have thus far produced."[58] In early 1926 Dreiser agreed to write an introduction to the Macmillan edition of *Lilith*, in which he called the play "as rare and gracious a form for the stage as that elusive platform has ever known."[59]

However, Sterling did not cultivate the acquaintance of only famous writers of the 1920s. Part of his role as the major San Francisco literary figure was to provide assistance to younger writers. This he did graciously and selflessly, sometimes passing on lucrative commissions to others and always giving encouragement and critical help to those who asked him. Typical of this aspect of his professional life was his work on the Book Club of California's anthology of West Coast poets. Bender had asked him in 1923 to share the editing responsibilities with the poets Genevieve Taggard and James Rorty. As scrupulous as ever with the work of lesser-known poets, Sterling not only read every poem that was submitted, but also reread with extra care the poems that were rejected by his coeditors. A poem that all three became immediately enthusiastic about was "Continent's End," by an obscure Carmel poet, Robinson Jeffers.

When James Rorty went east in early 1925 he took Jeffers's *Tamar* with him and persuaded Mark Van Doren and Babette Deutsche to read it. The three published glowing reviews of the book in the *New York Herald Tribune*, the *New Republic*, and the *Nation*. Peter Boyle's edition sold out instantly, and in November 1925 Boni and Liveright bought out Jeffers's *Roan Stallion, Tamar, and Other Poems*, with Sterling's endorsement in the flyleaf.

Meanwhile, Sterling had insisted that the Book Club of California's anthology be entitled *Continent's End*; furthermore, he introduced Jeffers's work to many friends, including Albert Bender the philanthropist. And at a party given by his old friend Harry Lafler, Sterling presented Jeffers's manuscript of the dramatic poem "The Tower beyond Tragedy" and insisted that the guests read the entire play in parts. The poet and critic Benjamin De Casseres was present; extremely impressed by the poem, he became Jeffers's most enthusiastic admirer.

Sterling became a frequent visitor to the Jeffers cottage in Carmel, and until his death in 1926 he was one of Jeffers's few personal friends. To Sterling, Jeffers was the poet he might have become, and the fact that he lived in Carmel only made this more pointed. In the pamphlet he wrote for Boni and Liveright, *Robinson Jeffers: The Man and the Artist* (1926), he described Jeffers as a man "with the sternest, most searching blue-gray eyes that I have ever seen in a human face—a gaze more piercing than even that of Bierce's. In short, a more austere version of the Greek."[60] Sterling's pun on his own nickname, his numerous references to Bierce in the pamphlet, and his praise of qualities he sought to achieve in his own poetry, all suggest his identification with Jeffers. Sterling must have felt that if he had been able to adopt a style of life as indifferent to society as Jeffers's, he might have been a better poet. In late 1924 he wrote and published as a pamphlet a poem in imitation of Jeffers with a theme of incest called *Strange Waters*. It was clear even to him, however, that his style could never adapt enough to be other than a poor parody of Jeffers.

Despite his inability to write in the modern mode, Sterling's muse was very active during the 1920s. That period saw the publication of his verse dramas, *Lilith, Truth,* and *Rosamund; Selected Poems* (1923); a volume of poems entitled *Sails and Mirage* (1921); and a body of uncollected verse which was published posthumously in *After Sunset* (1939). Many magazines and reviews carried his poems and short stories, and he took over the poetry column in the *Overland Monthly,* entitling it, appropriately, "Rhymes and Reactions." From this forum he would assail the Imagists, the flappers, and the bankers, and ever more frequently would publish verses glorifying death.

He was often openly despondent in these years, and friends remarked later that he would speak of "joining Carrie." Joan London remembered that he kept always in his pocket a white envelope on which he had written "Peace," and his friend and lover Rose Travis was worried enough to take his cyanide away from him several times.[61] He always bought more. His health had begun to deteriorate noticeably—largely because of drinking. A binge now would end with Sterling in the hospital exhausted and agonized with terrible stomach pains.

For the most part he was able to control his drinking during 1925 and 1926; but when visiting literary friends came to town, he fell off the wagon with a vengeance, often spending the next week in the hospital. The visits of Edgar Lee Masters in March 1925 and his Carmel friend Sinclair Lewis in February 1926 marked two of the more painful celebrations. Sterling was beginning to pay for his pleasures with ever greater intervals of pain.

Sterling was delighted, however, when Mencken announced another visit to San Francisco. Planning for a grand celebration, Sterling spent days on end scouring the Bay area for pre-Prohibition liquor. His industry paid off, and soon his room in the Bohemian Club looked like the storeroom of a speakeasy, with the dust carefully left undisturbed on dozens of bottles. But, unaccountably, Mencken was delayed in Los Angeles, where he was visiting the writer Joseph Hergesheimer. Days stretched into weeks, and still Mencken failed to arrive. Sterling was always a very impatient man, and when he felt he could stand it no longer, he sampled some of the vintages he had collected.

When Mencken finally arrived on November 16, he found Sterling unable to leave his room. He wrote to Upton Sinclair the next day: "Poor George Sterling is in bed here, and seems to be very ill. He accumulated a large stock of bootleg liquors against my coming, and incautiously tried some samples. The result was a dreadful drunk. He looks to me to be in a really serious condition. I am thoroughly glad I wasn't here when he began."[62] That evening the official dinner for Mencken took place with Sterling still unable to move from his room. After the dinner Mencken went to see him, but Sterling did not answer his knock. At noon the next day the manager opened the door with his passkey, and found that Sterling had taken cyanide.

He left no note. Sometime before his death he had burned a number of papers in his room; still legible on two scraps of paper were some lines from *Lilith*: "Deeper into the darkness can I peer than most, yet find the darkness still beyond," and "I walk with phantoms that ye know not."[63] The body was cremated, and there was an elaborate funeral, attended by so many weeping women that one newsman callously dubbed them "the Committee." And at Newbegin's Bologna Café that night, all the patrons stood while the orchestra played Debussy's *L'Apres-midi d'un Faun.*[64]

Sterling's death accords well with what he had written about suicide, especially in the despairing passages of *Lilith* and in the essay "Pleasure and Pain." Surely the events of his last years provide insight into his motives: Bierce, London, and Carrie Sterling had sought the same form of release from pain and disillusionment, and he had as many personal disappointments as had they—poverty, failing health, loss of reputation, an increasing sense of having lived beyond his time. But beyond these, Sterling's suicide came as a result of long unresolved contradictions.

Upton Sinclair wrote that Sterling was killed by the nebular hypothesis—a silly oversimplification, but containing an element of truth. A cosmic perspective which led him to believe in the radical insignificance of men did little to counteract Sterling's disillusionment. Furthermore, his adherence to an ideal of art which rejected living things in favor of illusion and death and his urge to live according to the Bohemian ideal of life as art may have contributed to the obsession with suicide which darkened his later years. The ambivalence of his stance as a rebel from society—efforts to break free from the bourgeois contradicted by the need to achieve public recognition—may have led him to the conclusion that death is the ultimate Bohemia.

Sterling's suicide is of course not unique; many like him have sought to die for the same reasons. For example, in the eighth chapter of *Exile's Return*, his fine personal history of the "Lost Generation," Malcolm Cowley recounts the events leading to the suicide of the young poet Harry Crosby. Crosby and a young woman were found in New York's Hotel des Artistes in 1929, victims of an apparent suicide pact. After the immediate furor had subsided, Harry Crosby's death became an archetype for an alienated generation, symbolic of "the suicide of a whole order with which he had been identified."[65] In his book, Cowley uses the story of Crosby's death in just that way; in the isolated act of a not very talented poet he identifies a series of motifs which are duplicated in the lives of many of Crosby's contemporaries: "bohemianism, the religion of art, the escape from society, the effort to defend one's individuality even at the cost of sterility and madness, then the final period of demoralization when the whole philosophical structure crumbled from within, just at the moment when bourgeois society seemed to crumble after its greatest outpouring of luxuries, its longest debauch...."[66]

It should be clear that Sterling's suicide can be seen in much the same light. The religion of art, the uncertain socialism, the odd tension between rebelling against bourgeois society and catering to the bourgeois taste for sensationalism—these elements form as much of Sterling's life as of Crosby's, and lead to the same self-destructiveness. And in this context it is significant that the lives of many of Sterling's companions show the same pattern of alienation that was typical of the American expatriates of the next generation. Merely to list the suicides among Sterling's acquaintances would indicate the parallel: there were Nora May French in 1907, Ambrose Bierce in 1914, Jack London in 1916, and Carrie Sterling in 1918. To this group can be added others: aside from Sterling's boyhood friend the boxer Pete McCoy, there were Bierce's son Day; Eduardo Scott, an artist who killed himself in 1919; Betty de Jong, a French painter who shot herself in a San Francisco studio in 1920; and Herman Scheffauer, Bierce's other favorite pupil, who killed himself and his mistress in a Berlin hotel in 1927, in an episode strangely similar to the death of Harry Crosby. And the list could easily be longer.

Sterling's friends who committed suicide had several things in common· they were all of an older generation than Harry Crosby; except for Scheffauer they were not personally involved in the war; and except for McCoy they were all artistic. And although the personal motives for an act as complex as suicide vary tremendously, the point must still remain that the contradictions Cowley discusses with reference to the writers of the 1920s were devastatingly real to the earlier expatriates who sought "another country" in Carmel cottages and in San Francisco studios

But Sterling's life is more than an exemplum of the self-destructive condition of the artist in America. He lived beyond the prewar Bohemia in which he had been most at home, yet he was never pathetic; there was always a kind of integrity that transcended his personal faults and artistic failures. Despite her negative opinion of his poetry, Harriet Monroe admired him as the least egotistical of poets, and his dealings with other writers were almost always motivated by friendship rather than selfishness. It may be as a Bohemian that Sterling will be best known, but as a poet he made a contribution of his own. The range of Sterling's poetic achievement, and his role in the dramatic changes that took place in American poetry during his lifetime, will be the subject of the following chapters.

CHAPTER 3

Prophet of the Suns

I *American Literary Taste: The 1890s*

ONE of the commonplaces of Victorian criticism—that "authors were a modern priesthood whose duty was to 'enlighten and encourage and purify public opinion' "[1]—is at least as applicable to American letters at the turn of the century. The great nineteenth-century literary periodicals, though in a period of decline, were still regarded as sanctuaries of culture. Their editors, men like Henry Mills Alden of *Harper's Monthly* and Richard Watson Gilder of the *Century*, wielded their blue pencils freely in the effort "not to print anything that could not be read by the women of the family circle."[2] Thus the priestly role of the American man of letters was largely proscriptive; literature should uplift and improve society, but above all it should not offend. The final achievement of the literary custodians of culture, to many cultural historians, was the creation in those august and respected magazines of "an air of high-class mediocrity "[3] occasionally relieved by a page of Howells, James, or Twain. By 1900 the naturalists Norris, Dreiser, and Crane had begun to challenge this genteelism in the novel, but poetry remained completely in its sway.

The poems which appeared in the best periodicals were characterized by traditional Romantic motifs of escape, antiquarianism, primitivism, and the supremacy of Beauty. But almost universally Romanticism supplied merely a stance or a choice of subject, because it was subordinated to genteel requirements of refinement, good manners, pleasant didacticism, and sentimentality. A glance through E. C. Stedman's *American Anthology* (1900) supports the point: the poets of the close of the century display generous quantities of optimism, conventional piety, and

62

sentiment, but not, unfortunately, of originality or skill. Nearly all of the poems are imitations of British models; Stedman was right when he remarked in his introduction, "We have a twilight interval, with minor voices and their tentative modes and tones."[4] Among the most popular poets were the moralizing ex-minister Henry Van Dyke, the effusive Ella Wheeler Wilcox, and of course James Whitcomb Riley, the "bard of Indiana." Riley's advice to the Kentucky poet Madison Cawein summarizes his personal formula: "Keep 'em [poems] all sunny and sweet and wholesome clean to the core, or if ever tragic, with sound hopes ultimate, if pathetic, my God! with your own tears baptized and made good as mirth!"[5] Riley mined his particular vein of dialect and pathos with great success in the 1890s, and he had a host of imitators who tried to capture the public as Riley had with "The Old Man and Jim":

> The surgeon turnin' away with tears
> 'At hadn't leaked for years and years,
> As the hand of the dyin' boy clung to
> His father's, the old voice in his ears,—
> "Well, good-bye, Jim:
> Take keer of yourse'f!"[6]

When, on the other hand, poets attempted ideality, or a mood of spiritual searching, more often than not they equated the ideal with the imprecise. A pronounced characteristic of the loftier poems of the period is a tendency to use deliberately vague symbols which assumedly embody great truths, but actually communicate a sense of confusion. These lines by Philip Henry Savage are representative:

> I think of thee, and as the crystal bowl
> Is broken, and the waters of the soul
> Go down to death within the crystal sea,
> I faint and fail when (thou, the perfect Whole)
> I think of thee.[7]

A Brown University graduate student, C. T. Kindilien, read hundreds of volumes of American poetry published in the 1890s, and the first chapter of his dissertation on the topic established a "composite volume" as a format to which the average poet of the times conformed quite closely. Kindilien's typical volume of poetry contained the following: "a stereotyped title, a laudatory or self-effacing preface, a moral or didactic poem, one discussing religion more concretely, a nature description, a sentimental verse, one idealizing womanhood, a humanitarian reflection, a patriotic poem and one or more tributes to famous men."[8] These were, he reflected, the only possible types of poems which publisher and reader would accept.

Popular taste was equally limited with respect to earlier poetic voices. The "Fireside Poets," Lowell, Whittier, and Longfellow, were highly respected in the 1890s, but Whitman had fallen out of favor because of his "fleshly" quality, and Poe's influence was stronger in France than in the United States. Melville's poems were forgotten, and Emily Dickinson was largely misunderstood.

Predictably, the best of the contemporary poets of the 1890s were obscure. Crane's startling and innovative *Black Riders* had failed to gain an audience. Edwin Arlington Robinson was working in almost complete obscurity, railing against the "little sonnet-men . . ./Who fashion, in a shrewd mechanic way, songs without souls. . . ."[9] The Harvard poets, Stickney, Moody, Lodge, and Santayana, actually succeeded in portraying their fitful search for values in a world of increasing spiritual darkness, but they found no significant audience outside the readers of the *Harvard Monthly*. Even the little Bohemian magazines of the decade, *Yellow Book* imitators like *M'lle New York* and the *Chap-Book*, had to restrict themselves to translations of foreign material when they wished to convey a *fin-de-siècle* air of decadence. As Kindilien remarks, any poet of the 1890s who ignored the demands of genteelism that poetry be sentimental, entertaining, and moralizing would have to give up the dream of reaching a public.[10]

Such was the literary situation when Sterling first began to seek advice from Ambrose Bierce, and in many ways Sterling's achievement will have to be measured against the poets of the "twilight interval" who were his true contemporaries.

II *Lessons of the Master*

By the time that Sterling met him, Ambrose Bierce was the acknowledged "Rhadamanthus of West Coast letters." It was generally understood among local literati that "no man's reputation as a writer was quite made until Bierce had pronounced on him."[11] From his "Prattle" column in the *San Francisco Examiner* Bierce would praise the few and censure the many, with scathing invective in the best tradition of personal journalism. For example: "[Mr. Harrison] loved to roll on the Parnassian Mount,/His pen to suck and all his thumbs to count";[12] and "I am seldom thrashed by poets without feeling my position keenly. Still if he [Mr. Lezinsky] must use his hand either to thrash me or write verses the public will find me faithful to duty and ready for the sacrifice."[13] Given the manifest power of Bierce's role as literary arbiter for the Pacific Coast region, it is not surprising that young writers sought his regard. Yet the group of avid tyros who gathered around Bierce were motivated by more than the need to curry favor with the critic whose pen could ruin them.

It seems that Bierce possessed an uncommon degree of personal magnetism. Nearly all of his acquaintances noted the striking physical presence of the man, whose military bearing and biting blue eyes commanded attention in any group. Sterling himself remarked, "His whole personality gave the impression of rugged strength and extreme vitality. Indeed, I have heard one young woman declare, 'I can feel him ten feet away!' "[14] To be sure, young women of indifferent talent comprised the majority of Bierce's disciples—despite his well-known misogyny. Yet Bierce attracted talented writers of both sexes who were captivated by his personal charm, his reputation as a man of letters, and his authoritarian air of complete critical certainty.

It is probably significant that none of the adoring pupils who addressed Bierce as "Dear Master," "Grossmeister," "Magister," and even "Thor" achieved lasting fame, and only Gertrude Atherton, Edwin Markham, and George Sterling acquired contemporary distinction. There is a discernible pattern in Bierce's relations with his pupils; a neophyte whose talents were newly discovered would please, especially if he or she displayed complete acquiescence. But inevitably would come the pupil's realization that Bierce would brook no disagreement and, worse, would permit little independence of thought, and the relationship would end in mutual disillusionment and bitterness. If one did not agree in all major respects with the master, the penalty—sooner or later—was banishment.

For example, at a party on New Year's Eve, 1898, Bierce's protégé Edwin Markham read a new poem which he had entitled "The Man with the Hoe." The literary editor of the *Examiner*, Bailey Millard, was so moved by the poem that he published it with great fanfare in the January 15 issue of his paper, and it became famous overnight. Bierce, miffed that someone else should so loudly "discover" one of his own pupils, and outraged at Markham's socialism, derided the poem in his column: "The notion that the sorrows of the humble are due to the selfishness of the great is 'natural,' and can be made poetical, but it is silly. As a literary conception it has not the vitality of a sick fish."[15] He immediately renounced his friendship for both Millard and Markham (though Millard later returned to his good graces). Furthermore, the popularity of the work incensed him, and he returned several times in print to his diatribe against the "poem which, despite some of its splendid lines, is neither true in sentiment nor admirable in form—which is, in fact, addressed to peasant understandings and soured hearts."[16] He execrated its diction, notably the use of the "agricultural implement"—"hoe" being too low a word for the decorum of serious verse. And he denounced Markham personally: "in the smug prosperity that he reviles in others, his great gift 'shrinks to its second cause and is no more.' "[17]

A great deal about Bierce's aesthetics can be deduced from his attack on Markham's poem. First, it is clear that he held rather conservative views on poetic diction and poetic subject-matter. The "hoe" was too humble an "implement," and the farmer was too debased to be a proper poetic subject. It is not surprising, then, to find in Bierce's collected literary criticism a number of philippics against dialect poetry and substandard English in general. Dialect, according to Bierce, is the "loutly locution of an illiterate clown making a trial at his mother-speech."[18] The only proper value of dialect might be to the "hardy philologer tracing backward the line of linguistic evolution to the grunt of the primeval pig."[19] A dialect poet like James Whitcomb Riley "affects the sensibilities like the ripple of buttermilk falling into a pig-trough."[20] In fact, to Bierce there was a positive correlation between the quality of language and that of thought, and between grammatical propriety and the level of civilization: "The fight against faulty diction is a fight against insurgent barbarism—a fight for high thinking and right living—for art, science, power—in a word, civilization."[21]

Second, Bierce's attack on Markham's Socialist views is a reflection not only of his intense personal bias against any leftist political stance, but also of his aesthetics. The "first cause" of poetry is beauty; no other is possible. Bierce rejected without compromise the didactic element of contemporary verse, to the extent that he excluded even a poetry of ideas: "it is the philosopher's trade to make us think, the poet's to make us feel."[22]

But if the poet's primary task is to make us feel, Bierce placed severe restrictions on what sort of feelings are permissible. So great was his disdain of the sentimentality which prevailed in American poetry that he inveighed against any excess of "human interest" to the exclusion of "art." Too "human" a tone, he argued, threatened to detract from the sublimity of the finest poetry; if poems have too much personality, they might easily lapse into the commonplace.

Yet Bierce believed that great poetry is the highest achievement of any civilization, and ignoring the contradictions, he asserted, "I should say that the greatest man is the man capable of doing the most exalted, the most lasting and the most beneficial intellectual work—and highest, ripest, richest fruit of the human intellect, is indubitably great poetry."[23] For Bierce, the only test of great poetry is the judgment of history, and history ultimately upholds poetry above other works of man: "Literature and art are all that the world really cares about in the end; those that make them are not without justification in regarding themselves as masters in the House of Life and all others as their servitors."[24] Contemporary judgments are useless, if not completely distorting: "There is not a true poet in this country who has not experienced the deep disgust of observing the 'popularity' of his own worst work."[25] Therefore, a poet who is sure of his gift must ignore the opinion of the vulgar masses in favor of the judgment of the noble few who can see beyond the petty limitations of their times. He must hold his art aloof from the petty squabblings of his fellows, and write for the ages.

In his adoration of Poe, his absolute rejection of didacticism, his fondness for the grotesque, and his belief in the supremacy of the purely aesthetic dimensions of poetry, Bierce was closer to the European Decadence than most of his fellow American critics. And if his remarkably proscriptive views made it difficult for his pupils to develop under his tutelage, there is no question that his influence helped them counteract "the sentimentality and absurdity which frequently steal upon the young American writer," as his protégé Herman Scheffauer put it.[46] The effect of these views on George Sterling, as we shall see, was profound.

For several years, Sterling was one of the Bierce coterie without distinguishing himself. But unlike most of the others, he had a felicity of language that made it possible for him to adapt to Bierce's standards, and he had the ability to sustain his creative work in Bierce's absence. After his mentor moved permanently to Washington, D.C., in 1899, Sterling became Bierce's most favored protégé. Probably the geographical distance made it possible for him to avoid for so long the fate of "banishment." His interests in socialism and a Bohemian style of life, both inimical to Bierce, did not often intrude on their relationship, and Sterling was able to remain the devoted neophyte for a while—by mail.

From the first, Bierce's attitude toward Sterling was a curious mixture of asperity and indulgence. For example, in December 1900 Sterling sent Bierce some sonnets for perusal. Bierce's response: "Why do most of 'you youngsters' tackle the sonnet? The same reason neophyte actors want to play Hamlet."[27] After four years, Sterling was still too much the neophyte to attempt the sonnet. And in the first few months of 1901, Bierce felt constrained to recommend an anthology of American verse (January 1), to show the differences between the rhyme schemes of Petrachan, Shakespearean, and "modern English" sonnets (February 7), and to recommend as basic a resource as *Roget's Thesaurus* (May 2). It must be concluded that Sterling was

still fairly ignorant of his craft. Yet Bierce was able to say on
February 17, "You grow great so rapidly that I shall not much
longer dare to touch your work. I mean that."[28]

The earliest Sterling manuscript in existence is *The Sea Waif*,
a blank-verse narrative of little poetic merit. Bierce's marginal
comments, however, are revelatory: because the poem lacked a
narrative line, he remarked that Sterling should "supply some
of the *story*." However, he went on to say that it was "*poetical*
all through, and some of the lines are exceedingly felicitous—
many of them."[29] Three lines were found worthy of special
praise: "Grey, glabrous, fat with all the sunken dead," and
"Black in the molten portals of the sun,/But crowned with one
keen pinnacle of light."[30]

The lines are representative of Bierce's standard because of
three qualities: their grotesqueness, an effect which Bierce's
stories often utilize; their supercharged, elevated imagery, which
lacks naturalistic detail; and their complete lack of sentiment.
These characteristics would always be noticeable in Sterling's
poetry, and they are directly attributable to Bierce's influence.
To be didactic, Bierce taught, is to reduce the poem to a commonplace moral statement rather than the evocation of imperish-
able beauty that it ought to be. In fact, "horror is an aspect of
beauty, perhaps greater than any other,"[31] he told Sterling on
one occasion. Poetry should escape from the commonplace into
the mysterious, to the borders of the inexpressable.

In April 1901 Sterling sent Bierce a longer poem called
"Memorial Day, 1901." Bierce thought highly enough of this
effort that he refused to alter it. Furthermore, he tried to have
it published in the *Journal*. When he was unsuccessful he published the poem in his own column in the *Washington Post*. This
was the first time that Sterling had secured publication, and it
was the beginning of a practice of "literary logrolling" on Bierce's
part which would secure for Sterling a national reputation, but
would lead to controversy about Sterling's merits.

The poem "Memorial Day, 1901" shows how strongly Bierce's
influence had molded him in the earliest stages of his career as
a published poet. It also shows some of the limits of that influence. In a typical comment about poetry and ideas, Bierce wrote
to Sterling, "Somebody has defined poetry as 'glorious nonsense.'

It is not an altogether false definition, albeit I consider poetry the flower and fruit of speech, and would rather write gloriously than sensibly. But if poets saw things as they were, they would write no more poetry."[32] Despite Bierce's objections, many of Sterling's poems are attempts to deal with "things as they are" rather than with "glorious nonsense."

The first stanzas of "Memorial Day" demonstrate that Sterling had inherited from the Victorians via Bierce a certain imprecision of imagery and artificiality of expression that make the meaning unclear:

> To each the city of his dream!
> Far lifts the purple of its walls,
> And pure its domes eternal gleam
> Above the promise of its halls.
>
> Unto each soul her chosen ways
> And travail upward from the night.
> Enough, that from her dark of days
> She have in quest the twisted light.[33]

The verses strain for nobility, but achieve only vagueness, a fault typical of the time. However, as one reads "Memorial Day" he realizes that behind all the forced and clichéd grandeur, Sterling is trying to articulate some thoughts on the nature of human progress.

The poem presents two basic possibilities for peace. There is the peace of the dead, and the peace of a future without war, "submissive to a deeper word" of human or divine justice. The second possibility is expanded into most of the poem, a portrayal of the "diviner cities" of a possible future. There is an allusion to the Idea of Progress, "the heights of 'freedom whereunto/We dream the toiling ages trend." Resplendent with the works of love and of art, this future civilization will be possible, however, only as a product of war and only because of the vigilance of its defenses against the forces of brutality and violence. Therefore, the Idea of Progress with its vision of future peace is negated. The vision of the future fades into a tribute to the dead soldiers who have defended civilization; and then the dreamlike slumber of death is presented as a truer and more immutable kind of peace than any dream of future utopias.

The thoughts here, though derivative in other ways, show independence from the dicta of Bierce. The pessimism and the glorification of death are themes Bierce no doubt approved of, but he would not necessarily have recommended that the question of human progress be treated poetically. Sterling, then, was beginning to move away from complete dependence on Bierce's judgment. His experiences, his reading, and the influence of his friends were placing him in conflict with Bierce on small points; and as he began to associate more with Socialists, the conflicts grew.

Evidence of this growing concern over the relation of art to social purpose can be found as early as October 1901, when Sterling sent Bierce a poem which addresses itself directly to the problem. The poem, entitled "To Ambrose Bierce," is really a tribute to Sterling's mentor; and as such it reaffirms a tenet of the Bierce aesthetic; the poet should concern himself not with the trivial strivings of men, but with beauty in its most eternal and indeed inhuman aspect:

> Her [the Muse's] altars lift incessant fire;
>> She holds no truce with Death or Peace;
>> Till mind degrade and beauty cease,
> She calls her chosen to the Lyre.
>
> Remiss the ministry they bear
>> Who serve her with divided heart.
>> She stands, reluctant to impart
> Her strength to purpose, end, or care. (pp. 7–8)

And yet, the poet insists, the temptations of the "divided heart" are not easy to resist. Is it possible for the poet to serve beauty and fight against injustice at the same time? For that matter, how can the poet remain unconcerned while men struggle in the "slime of oppression" without an "advocate/to cry their wrongs"?

The poem moves on to question the tenets which it began by affirming. What value is art if it must disdain humanity?

Despite the fact that it is a tribute to Bierce, the poem becomes
a forum for some of Sterling's skepticism about his role as a
poet:

> So questioning, can I endure
>   The peace of mine uplifted place?
>   Accused and judge, I fear to face
> The dumb tribunals of the poor. (p. 10)

As if in recognition of his own boldness to question Bierce so
openly, Sterling wrote beneath the stanza: "I suppose the above
rhyme is *barely* permissible—or no?"[34] The skepticism of the
poem is extended at this point: Sterling questions the benevo-
lence of the God who could allow these evils to exist. But such
questionings are beyond the powers of the poet's "unequal"
spirit. He must attempt, resignedly, the tragic order of things,
and when possible, he must rely on the fuller understanding of
thinkers like Bierce, which may make it possible for him to find
deeper truth than he is capable of discovering alone:

> Emotion smites with blinded aim;
>   Religion seeks, a baffled wraith,
>   The ignis fatuus of faith,
> And learning tends a ruthless flame.
>
> I, fearful of Unreason's drink,
>   Avail me of a deeper sight,
>   And turn me to thy clearer light,
> In which as babes we others blink. (pp. 11–12)

Bierce was flattered by the poem, and responded that if it
had been addressed to anyone other than himself, he would
say that it was exceptionally "printable."[35] The poem's ending
indicates how completely Sterling was willing to subordinate
himself to Bierce's judgment. His admiration for Bierce approached idolatry, and certainly included an overvaluation of
his tutor's wisdom. It was years, for instance, before Sterling
would admit that Bierce's pessimism "was of a sophomoric
order."[36]

Even though Sterling resolved the conflict in his poem with

a tribute to Bierce, the latter was still disturbed by its socialism, implied in such lines as "the dumb tribunals of the poor." Oddly enough, he did not recommend that Sterling cut or change the offending lines, as he did with a stanza which employed the image of "fatherhood" too suggestively for his taste. Instead, he cautioned Sterling very seriously against socialism and against those of his friends who would lead him "in the dirty paths . . . of social and political 'reform' ": "Don't fiddle-faddle with such infinitesimal and tiresome trivialties as (for example) the immemorial squabbles of 'rich and poor' on this 'mote in the sun-beam.' (both 'classes,' when you come to that, are about equally disgusting and unworthy—there's not a pin's moral difference between them). Let them cheat and pick pockets and cut throats to the satisfaction of their base instincts, but do thou regard them not. . . . 'Settle' it how they will—another beat of the pendulum and all as before; and ere another, man will again be savage, sitting on his naked haunches and gnawing raw bones."[37]

Sterling's Socialist leanings would create a constant source of tension in his relations with Bierce. As he became more a public figure in California, and as his relationships with writers like Jack London strengthened, the disapproval of Bierce became more and more vehement. One of the basic conflicts in his own attitude toward his work, likewise, was the division between, as Lionel Stevenson puts it, "the impulses of romantic escape and humanitarian dedication."[38] But the conflict was put aside temporarily and Bierce's irritation disappeared when, in March 1902, Sterling sent him the first draft of "The Testimony of the Suns."

III *"The Testimony of the Suns"*

Sterling's "star poem" was composed over a period spanning several months. After Sterling submitted to Bierce the draft of the first part of the poem in March 1902, the two exchanged letters and drafts with revisions suggested by Bierce or volunteered by Sterling. From the first, Bierce was dazzled by the new poem: "It is a new field, the broadest yet discovered. To paraphrase Coleridge, 'you are the first that ever burst/Into

that silent (unknown) sea'—A silent sea *because* no one else has
burst into it in full song. True, there have been short incursions
across the 'border,' but only by way of episode. The tremendous
phenomena of Astronomy have never had adequate poetic treatment, their meaning adequate expression. You must make it
your own domain. You shall be the poet of the skies, the prophet
of the suns."[39]

Lately Sterling had been reviving his boyhood interest in
astronomy, and he had decided to treat galactic phenomena in
a long poem, at the same time dealing with some philosophical
and moral problems posed by science. In this respect he was of
course following a Victorian poetic tradition, but in the poem
he would assault Victorian morality and spiritual doubt from a
consistent perspective of cosmic determinism.

Two contemporary writers, Ernst Haeckel and H. G. Wells,
were direct influences on Sterling's poem. Haeckel, the German
biologist who was one of the chief survivors among the early
Darwinians, had published in 1899 a work of popular philosophy
entitled *Die Welträtsen.* Translated into English in 1900 as
The Riddle of the Universe, the book was enormously popular
in the United States among the intellectual avant-garde.[40]
Haeckel repudiated traditional concepts of a personal God, an
immortal soul, and a free human will; consequently, his work
was a strong influence on naturalists like Dreiser.

In his "law of substance," Haeckel combines the laws of
conservation and energy into a single principle, which in turn
implies an infinitely extended universe of eternal duration and
transformation: ". . . in the collision of two heavenly bodies
which rush towards each other at inconceivable speed, enormous quantities of heat are liberated, while the pulverized
masses are hurled and scattered about space. The eternal drama
begins afresh—the rotating mass, the condensation of its parts,
the formation of new meteorites, their combination into larger
bodies and so on."[41]

If Haeckel had introduced to Sterling the conception of a
cosmic storm far beyond human perceptions, it was H. G. Wells
who first showed him some of the imaginative possibilities of
the theme. In 1904 he wrote to Wells that "The Testimony of
the Suns" had been partly inspired by the short story "Under

the Knife." In this tale, the narrator is undergoing an operation and is near death when he has a vision of his soul spinning through space and time: "Stars glowing brighter and brighter with their circling planets catching the light in a ghostly fashion as I neared them, shone out and vanished again into inexistence; faint comets, clusters of meteorites, winking specks of matter, eddying light-points, whizzed past, some perhaps a hundred millions of a mile or so from me at most, few nearer, travelling with unimaginable rapidity, shooting constellations, momentary darts of fire, through that black, enormous night."[42] Wells's story showed Sterling the way in which a sublime poetry could be written about the stars—poetry that would both fit the Bierce formula and as well convey Sterling's own naturalism, influenced by Haeckel.

In its final version, "The Testimony of the Suns" has two parts, containing in all 162 four-line stanzas, rhymed in the *In Memoriam* manner. Part I describes the "war" of the stars in the cosmos, and Part II attempts to relate human life to that universal war. The poem opens with a contrast between the perspective of "Time," or the temporal vision of man, and "Eternity," or the absolute vision of universal law. "In the eyes of time," then, the evening skies seem peaceful, intransigent, and beyond all human conflict. But to the eyes of Eternity, the skies are a vast battleground: the stars are at war; their movements are such that one will inevitably collide with another, causing it to disintegrate into a nebula or dead star. In the eternal flux of the cosmos, however, nebulae eventually evolve into new stars. Thus, there is an external process of creation and destruction in the heavens, quite remote from human concerns, and so alien to human time that it takes a supreme intellectual effort even to conceptualize it.

In describing these wars in the heavens, Sterling uses two primary types of imagery. One, naturally enough, is martial:

> O armies of eternal night,
>> How flame your guidons on the dark!
>> Silent we turn from Time to hark
> What final Orders sway your might. (p. 44)

Another common source of imagery is the sea:

> The war whose waves of onslaught, met
> Where night's abysses storm afar,
> Break on the high, tremendous bar
> Athwart that central ocean set— (p. 44)

In many stanzas of the poem, Sterling exploits the rhetorical effects which Bierce taught him to regard as "sublime." For example, several of them employ apostrophes to various stars; each of these is a slight variation on the same expression of wonder at the immense scope and mystery of the conflict:

> Altair, what captains compass thee?
> What foes, Aldebaran, are thine?
> Red with what blood of wars divine
> Glows that immortal panoply? (p. 45)

Dying and newly engendered stars are part of the spectacle of the night skies; "smit. suns . . . startle back the gloom" (p. 46), and the new light of the nova makes its way to the uncomprehending eyes of humanity. Do we believe that this maelstrom has a beginning and an ending? If we do, we are fools.

The mist of a nebula marks the collision of stars in some cosmic past; but the nebula will evolve to new suns, which will foster a reawakening life, the birth of reason, and the emergence of a civilization, until once again, there will be seen "The nearing sun's enormous disc,/Blood-red at dusk of sullen noon" (p. 49). Again, the collision of stars will create a new nebula, witnessed, perhaps, by the "barbaric eyes" (p. 50) of denizens of the worlds of Betelgeuse and Altair.

Sterling goes on at length to discuss the folly and vanity of those men who try to question the laws of the universe as science has revealed them. The delusions that men fall prey to can be grouped into two categories: the speculations that mankind is eternal, and the "dream of Faith" that there is a life beyond death. These are never to be fulfilled, because law is unalterable; and man is subject to the same law of destruction that controls the destinies of stars. Even if there is an apocalypse for man, it will certainly not bring the universe to an end:

> Shall Godhead dream a transient thing?
> Strives He for that which now he lacks?
> Shall Law's dominion melt as wax
> At touch of Hope's irradiant wing? (p. 59)

Would the Almighty be subject to whim? This is what men are asserting if they believe in any kind of human redemption. The first part of the poem ends on a note of "unfathomed mystery" (p. 63), preparing the reader for Part Two, in which Sterling intended to develop further the pathos of human attempts to anthropomorphize the universe.

It should be clear by now that "The Testimony of the Suns" has little attraction for the modern reader. It is filled with archaisms and overly "sublime" rhetorical effects, and it lacks precise statement of its ideas. It is difficult to elucidate such lines as these:

> Charged, the immeasured gulfs transmit
> Her [Law's] mandate to the fonts of life,
> Inciting to the governed strife
> Whereby the lethal voids are lit,
>
> With augment of imperious tides
> On vague, illimitable coasts,
> And battle-haze of merging hosts
> To which the flare of Vega rides. (p. 60)

The second part of the poem especially falls prey to these excesses. In the effort to sustain the grandeur, Sterling allows his stanzas to become strident and nearly hysterical at times, and at other times deadly monotonous:

> Reborn to that selective strife
> and fury of ascendant wars,
> What tidings of the immortal shores?
> What covenant from Death, O Life?

When, in what maze of spacial bound,
    Or cryptic glooms that wall the grave,
    Hast heard the secret which we crave
From that inscrutable Profound?

What surety that thy sons attain
    The litten council of thy Lords,
    And thunder of seraphic chords
To music not of Time and Pain?

What whisper from the world new-born
    Recalled thy footsteps to essay
    The far, inevitable way
Lit sunward from thy mists of morn? (p. 72)

A major reason for the poem's failure to sustain interest is the counsel of Bierce. Afraid that Sterling would descend to the level of mere humanity in the second part of the poem, Bierce had written, "If you descend from Arcturus to Earth, from your nebulae to your neighbors, from life to lives, from the measureless immensities of space to the petty passions of poor insects, won't you incur the peril of anti-climax? I doubt if you can touch the 'human interest' after those high themes without an awful tumble. I should be sorry to see the poem 'Peter out' or 'soak in.' It would be as if Goethe had let his 'Prologue in Heaven' expire in a coon-song."[43] Accordingly, Sterling abandoned any plan he might have had to vary the perspective of his poem. Instead he wrote dozens of stanzas with the same basic ideas and rhetorical effects. Bierce approved entirely, and remarked in his marginal notes to the completed manuscript, "This grows better the more frequently it is read. It is as high a note as was ever struck—and held." His failure to encourage Sterling to develop a sense of restraint might have been the worst effect of his influence.

Behind the excesses of the rhetoric, however, is the revelation of a cosmic abyss, reinforced by the astronomical theme and leading only to despair:

O Space and Time and stars at strife,
    How dreadful your infinity!

> Shrined by your termless trinity
> How strange, how terrible, is life! (p. 75)

Humanity will always seek "to know what permanence abides/ Beyond the veil the senses draw" (p. 83). But there will be no revelations: men are trapped in time, and they will

> . . . crave unanswered, till, denied
> By cosmic gloom and stellar glare,
> The brains are dust that bore the pray'r
> And dust the yearning lips that cried. (p. 84)

The poem's final statement, then, is of "the impotence and eternal loneliness of human beings, involved in some vast and incomprehensible law of cyclic recurrence."[44] And thus, despite its flaws, "The Testimony of the Suns" is historically significant. Along with the then-forgotten poems of Stephen Crane and the still unknown poems of Robinson, it is one of the earliest naturalist poems in America. Almost Schopenhauerian in its emphasis upon the primacy of pain, it is in its way a remarkable poem for the "twilight interval" in which it was written. Bierce had helped make Sterling into a significant transitional figure— a poet whose nineteenth-century rhetoric and traditional stock of images contrast sharply with a very modern sense of despair.

Yet in "The Testimony of the Suns" the despair seems submerged in an exultant, almost joyous chanting—the catalogue of stars, the repeated questions—that remind us of Margaret Marshall's comment about Fitzgerald: "The gusto with which *This Side of Paradise* and *The Beautiful and the Damned* were written was clearly affirmative, though the theme was disintegration."[45] Like the young Fitzgerald, Sterling was reveling in his success. Bierce had called him "the prophet of the suns," and with this accolade he felt that he had found his voice and his theme.

IV "*A Poet of Keatsian Promise*"

George Sterling's first volume of poems displays both the unmistakable influence of Bierce and the range of his own lyric

gift. *The Testimony of the Suns and Other Poems* (1903) is far
from Kindilien's representative volume of turn-of-the-century
poetry. Didacticism and sentimentality are almost entirely absent, and the poems, though pervasively lyrical, are seldom
personal in tone or subject. The language is traditional and
erudite, and there are an abundance of classical and learned
allusions.

Aside from the "Memorial Day" poem already discussed, a
few lyrics deal with war. One is noteworthy because of its date
of composition, May 1, 1898, the first month of the Spanish-
American War. It describes the war as "our night of shame" at
the same time that it speculates that an unacknowledged and
uncontrolled larger fate of liberty may be working behind the
jingoism that has motivated the war. The "century-sun that sets
in blood" may well, however, bring another hundred years of
bloodshed:

> The Mother girds Her, glad to be
>   Where war's long surf of carnage beats.
>   E'en now her mighty breath awakes
> The first low thunder of that sea. (p. 104)

In a sonnet entiled "War," Sterling makes much the same comment: though once we hoped that the new century would bring
peace, it now is clear that the age will dawn crimson: "But
with the falling of the last red sands,/Like to a blooddrop
gleamed the morning-star . . ." (p. 108).

Some of the shorter poems are conventional love-lyrics, but
quite impersonal in tone: "To One Loved," "To a Lily," "To
My Wife," "Words for Lange's 'Blumenlied.'" In most of them,
it is fair to say, the loved one is not so important as the emotions
of the poet. For example, the sonnet "Reincarnation," a poem
about a lover who has died, ends with a speculation about
memory:

> Alas, if irretrievably we part . . .
>   The spirit boweth with her weight of fears.
>   Ah! met again within the farther years,
> Shall I not know thee for the ghost thou art?

Or will there be no wonder at the heart
And sudden starlight in remembering tears? (p. 120)

As one might expect from a disciple of Bierce, few poems in the volume deal with current or topical issues, and the lyrics which are concerned with personal feelings tend to idealize the emotions and therefore make them more abstract. The persona or speaking voice itself tends to be idealized into poet as cosmic seer, or poet as quivering sensibility.

Several poems are about flowers; the best of them is "A White Rose," a lyric in which Sterling uses the beauty of a flower as an occasion for metaphysical speculation, as he does later in his career in the ode "The House of Orchids." The fragile beauty of a rose occasions the fanciful conjecture of what it would be like to *be* a rose, whose patience, sweetness, and calmness attest to its complete acceptance of life. Then the realization emerges that a rose has a kind of "brother-life" to ours, alien, "remote from human time." This thought leads to a perception of the limited range of human awareness—"Our senses light a little arc." In a rare use of this sort of paradox, Sterling compares this limited light of man to the profound darkness of God,

Whose range of unrecorded night,
And distance of eternal plan,
Isle in equality of light
The stars of life in flower and man. . . . (p. 98)

For God, the life of a flower and that of a man may well be equal, and if there is reincarnation into various forms of life, perhaps the poet himself, in some future life, may attain the innocence of a rose.

Many other poems have metaphysical themes. "The Parting" (p. 122) describes the sorrowful separation of souls in a pre-existent state of unity, when one spirit assumes flesh and must abandon its mystic union with the others. Human love at its most ecstatic contains an echo of this old sorrow, because a loved one's face has the power to make us nearly remember that prenatal moment of parting. "The Fog Siren" (p. 36) describes the eerie moan of a foghorn over the coast as a

summoning of the ghosts of the drowned. Then, in a surprising
shift of tone, the foghorn's sound seems apocalyptic: "We hear,
upon the trembling of the deep,/The bellow of the Beast drawn
down to doom . . ." (p. 36). The fog becomes a strangely appropriate setting for that moment.

In anticipation of a concern of Sterling's later career, a theme
of pain-in-pleasure recurs throughout the volume. Two sonnets,
"The Swoon" and "The Lords of Pain" deal with physical pain.
The latter is biographically interesting as an early rationale for
suicide as an alternative to a death of aging: it would be better
to "put by the guerdon of the breath/As one grown weary in
a twilight land,/Whom Music leads to sleep, and sleep to
Death" (p. 35). And the attractiveness of death as an alternative to tragic knowledge is presented in a kind of cosmic perspective in "Nightmare":

> But thou, O Death! shalt feign no dream nor dawn,
>   Tho' aeons sunder the hermetic tomb,
>   And night annul the mausolean gloom—
> Nay! tho' contending sun to sun be drawn
>   In ruin the worlds diffused attest
>   To watchers round Arcturus, *I shall rest!* (p. 109)

Aside from the title poem. the most ambitious lyrics in *The
Testimony of the Suns and Other Poems* deal with Romantic,
neo-Platonic themes of beauty and inspiration. In all of these,
the emphasis is on the impossible, inexpressible beauty of which
we catch glimpses, but which truly belongs to a shadowy, far-
off realm beyond death; several of these poems, including "To
Imagination," "Poesy," and "The Ideal," stress the poet's calling
to capture as much of beauty's essence as possible, and to offer
its poor reflection to the world. One of the more extended of
these is "The Spirit of Beauty," a blank-verse lyric of forty-eight
lines. In a vision, Beauty appears to the dreaming poet:

>   As a mist she fled
> Before mine eyes enchanted; and her face
> Was like a lily hidden in holy dusks—
> Even such as gaze, in vision far from Time,

> From out the skies of dream land, being moons
> In slumber's realm of shadow. And her eyes
> Were great with griefs unsearchable, and gleamed
> Sorrow beyond them, like the larger dew
> Of Aidenn, having each Love's perfect star
> Mirrored therein. And with her came the hush
> That follows music dying, or its peace
> About all dead things beautiful. . . . (p. 110)

She speaks to him in words that he cannot understand, and her voice is followed by the silence that

> Lay sweeter than all harmony: therein
> Slept Music and her dreams, and there was set
> The silence that enfolds the ineffable. (p. 112)

The poem contains a common paradox in all of Sterling's poems that evoke an ideal. Perfection—here Beauty—is always seen as the absence of its opposite, and as such is always a negative attribute; the perfect language lacks words, the perfect beauty lacks substance, the perfect music is silence. Not only does the paradox convey a stock theme of Decadent poetry—that we only can catch a fleeting glimpse of Beauty, which is beyond perception and beyond the language to express it—it also betrays a risk that Sterling as lyricist was always taking: in his quest for language and imagery that could convey the essence of Beauty without its substance, he could very easily end up with nothing at all.

Of course, Sterling knew that. In a longer poem, a blank-verse ode of some 200 lines called "Music," he pursued the Absolute a little farther toward nothingness. "Music," a personified abstraction much like "Beauty" in the other poem, is an indistinct female figure: "Her face we have a little, but her voice/Is not of our imagining nor time . . ." (p. 85). In the first stanza or verse-paragraph, Sterling identifies her with the Ideal. She is immortal and cosmic, yet her home is deep within us. She seems to be "ghost/Of all past beauty" and in her most joyous aspect, sorrow seems imminent. In the verse-paragraphs that follow, the nature of music is explored, but on the most abstract level:

the sounds of nature "echo and forewhisper" her song; the great
poets Keats, Poe, Milton, Homer, and Shelley have been be-
witched by her. Her voice has found the chosen few, through
whom in turn she echoes forth beauty:

> Silent we wait
> Their telling of her glories, tho' their souls
> Go mad with stress of the ineffable,
> Yearning forever in their powerlessness
> To cry the wonder heard, the harmonies
> That surge upon them from her hidden deep. (pp. 88–89)

But music, Sterling continues, is the spirit of all pleasure and
beauty, and here he indulges in flights of allusion and imagery
in his attempt to describe her evocative powers:

> At her call
> We see again the living rose-and pearl
> Fabled of Paphos, and the hurry of doves.
> She with the wind awakened, we have heard,
> Or seem to hear, the chime of fairy feet,
> Spurning the sea-strewn jewels of the moon. . . . (p. 89)

But as the poet muses further, it seems to him that music's
happiest mood has constant sorrow at its center. All songs, no
matter how joyous, are ultimately lamentations which grieve
at the soul's separation from its eternal osurce. And Life herself
is a cosmic orphan—a lonely, blind victim of Change and Death:

> And home she hath not—nay, nor any rest.
> Waif of eternity, her sightless eyes
> Are dewed of the illimitable mists
> That clasp her. And her night is very strange. (p. 93)

Music's song to life is only of exile and the homelessness of the
soul. Finally however, the poem ends more hopefully, as the
speculation is made that music's ultimate and "unimagined"
harmonics await the "archangel races" of the "world's greet
evensong." Perhaps the veil may yet be lifted, and the Absolute

will reveal herself; but for the present we must suffer "the grief and rapture of that human dream" (p. 96).

There is a remarkable consistency in the way Sterling's most Platonic poems end on a note of profound sadness and loss. The transcendence for which we so desperately strive is not possible. The soul's raptures are always momentary and illusory, and the timeless realm of Beauty remains as distant as if the struggle to achieve it had never taken place. Also remarkable is the way the poems consistently identify the Ideal with death, the ultimate mystery which is both oblivion and the doorway to perfection. The mystical religion of beauty that these early poems express is very close to becoming a worship of death.

Thus *The Testimony of the Suns and Other Poems* shows conflicting tendencies in Sterling's early work, best summarized as the radical desire for absolute beauty, offset by the conviction that the Absolute is either unattainable or nonexistent. The dominant tones, therefore (aside from "Testimony"), are regret and melancholy. This sort of poetic stance, stemming simultaneously from a need for transcendence and a failure to find transcendent values, is rather typical of the European Decadence, but was quite uncommon in the United States at the turn of the century.

If Sterling's early poetry has an American affinity, it is with Poe. Many qualities attest to the similarity: the use of incantatory language, words whose connotative and evocative qualities try to convey a sense of heightened consciousness; the pervasive sense of an Absolute which reigns beyond the veil of the senses and which is available only fleetingly to mortal eyes, and then only in extraordinary states of awareness; the implicit worship of death; the tendency to express ideas obliquely, allowing them to be perceived more intuitively than rationally; the belief that music and poetry are ultimately one; and the conviction that art exists for its own sake, without "purpose, end, or care."[46] In fact, Bierce once remarked in an essay on "greatness" that the greatest American poets (indeed, the greatest Americans) were Edgar Allan Poe and George Sterling.[47]

Influenced by Poe and by English poets like Rossetti, Swinburne, and Shelley, Sterling's work was in some ways close to the Symbolist movement; yet he was no proto-Symbolist working in near obscurity on the Pacific coast. His work touches on many nineteenth-century traditions without completely belonging to any. His poetry and his thought display elements of Romantic idealism and Naturalistic materialism, a Symbolist tendency to see language as incantatory and the poem as a means of achieving higher consciousness, as well as an opposing tendency to personify and allegorize abstractions, as a Symbolist would not do. In many important ways, Sterling's early poetry is like the Decadents', and when in later volumes he begins to exploit the Decadent interest in neurosis and the Decadent impulse for personal degradation, the resemblance is stronger yet.

Certainly it was rare then for a young poet in America to adopt such standards. Bliss Carman and Richard Hovey, for example, the popular but aseptic poets of "Vagabondia," paid lip service to "art for art's sake," and allegedly were influenced by the Symbolists but really owed more to Kipling and Henly. They were no threat to the prevailing genteelism, but Sterling's pessimism was another matter. Thus, through Bierce's influence, through his own wide reading, and through the independent development of his art, Sterling had established links with the most vital poetic movements of nineteenth-century Europe and had become a very unusual American poet.

CHAPTER 4

An American Decadent

IF Sterling's early verses, published in *The Testimony of the Suns and Other Poems*, show affinities with the themes of the European Decadence, then his poems of the Carmel years display a very conscious exploitation of those themes. In fact, in the poems we will examine here, nearly every characteristic of Decadence can be found: the search for novelty, the interest in the exotic and unnatural, the aesthetic assumption that poetry is a means of enchantment, with a concurrent emphasis on language as an evocative and connotative instrument, the rhetorical ornamentation (resulting at times in a disintegration of artistic unity), the scorn of contemporary society, and the many allusions to an exotic past.[1]

I "A Wine of Wizardry"

As these qualities tend to pervade Sterling's work, others diminish. Certain forms disappear. Gone is the *In Memoriam* stanza as a vehicle for extended discourse on a serious theme (later in his career Sterling employs the ode and then the blank-verse drama for this purpose); also gone is the blank-verse meditation. But more important, gone forever are verses of metaphysical speculation which assume the existence of a spiritual realm. In *Testimony*, as we have seen, several lyrics— "A White Rose," "Reincarnation," and "The Soul's Exile," for example—display neo-Platonic themes of a preexistent harmony of the soul with the eternal spirit. Other lyrics—"Music," "The Spirit of Beauty"—present poetry and its sister art, music, as pathways to the divine realm. In Sterling's second book, *A Wine of Wizardry and Other Poems* (1909), these neo-Platonic lyrics are replaced by poems which reveal a deepening sense of loss

87

and abandonment (present in *Testimony* but not nearly as pervasive) and a desperate, often self-destructive sort of hedonism.

Sterling's shift to Decadence is very evident in the playful perversity of "A Wine of Wizardry," the poem which made him famous. In this long lyric, the dominant aesthetic principle seems to be that poetry is an exquisitely useless activity whose main function is to invoke extremes of sensation. The odd detachment of the poem would suggest that this is a rather effete sort of experimentation; yet the highly mannered language seems like a fabric stretched over an abyss of despair, hidden from the reader's view only by the gaudiness of that fabric.

As the poem begins, the speaker is drinking from a crystal goblet of red wine and musing into its depths. While he meditates, Fancy, a personification so abstract that she seems completely separate from his consciousness, "awakes with brow caressed by poppy-bloom," and wings her way to numerous bizarre and sinister scenes. Throughout the poem she remains unrealized except as a winged female figure, alternately fascinated, repelled, or disappointed by the various stages of her journey. As a dramatization of the visionary possibilities of the poetic sensibility heightened by wine, Fancy's very abstractness is a *fin-de siècle* version of transcendence, an attempt to explore imaginatively the possibilities of rapture-in-horror. Yet there is a sort of self-directed irony in the poem which generates not horror but humor. The imaginative journey is not so serious an attempt to explore sensation as it is an occasion for effects of imagery and color, and an opportunity for *épater le bourgeois* by being simply outrageous.

In the imagery of "A Wine of Wizardry," the visual element is predominant; and as in most of Sterling's descriptive poems, scenes are cast from a distance. Fancy's visits are made from afar, as befits such places as a grotto with "wattled monsters" and a "cowled magician," a polar iceberg with hidden sapphires, a battle of Titans against Olympians, a revel of Celtic elves, a Syrian treasure-house, and a multitude of other exotic and grotesque scenes. Through all of these visions with their varied splendors and horrors shines the ruddy glare of the red wine, until the entire poem seems suffused in a baleful, bloody light:

> And swarthy mariners from alien strands
> Stare at the red horizon, for their eyes
> Behold a beacon burn on evening skies,
> As fed with sanguine oils at touch of night.
> Forth from that pharos-flame a radiance flies
> To spill in vinous gleams on ruddy decks;
> And overside, when leap the startled waves
> And crimson bubbles rise from battle-wrecks,
> Unresting hydras wrought of bloody light
> Dip to the ocean's phosphorescent caves.[2]

Fancy seems to be in quest of new and thrilling sensations, as though the grotesque has become commonplace and only the perverse and excessive will bring the pleasure of discovery. The reader becomes dizzied by the rapid change of scene and the hothouse luxuriance of the imagery as Fancy quests onward, avoiding all resting places, repelled by what she sees, yet always in search of new horrors, like the chamber of the sorceress Circe:

> Carved in one ruby that a Titan lost,
> Where icy philters brim with scarlet foam,
> 'Mid hiss of oils in burnished caldrons tost,
> While thickly from her prey his life-tide drips,
> In turbid dyes that tinge her torture-dome,
> As craftily she gleans her deadly dews,
> With gyving spells not Pluto's queen can use,
> Or listens to her victim's moan, and sips
> Her darkest wine, and smiles with wicked lips. (p. 16)

Jaded, Fancy seeks other phantasmagoria, until the poem becomes overtly sadistic, when she visits hell:

> But Fancy still is fugitive, and turns
> To caverns where a demon altar burns,
> And Satan, yawning on his brazen seat,
> Fondles a screaming thing his friends have flayed,
> Ere Lilith come his indolence to greet,
> Who leads from hell his whitest queens, arrayed
> In chains so heated at their master's fire
> That one new-damned had thought their bright attire
> Indeed were coral. . . . (p. 17)

The visions whirl and sweep, ending with the two most outrageous (and notorious) lines in all of Sterling's poems:

> The blue-eyed vampire, sated at her feast,
> Smiles bloodily against the leprous moon. (p. 19)

This marks the end of Fancy's journey. With the onset of
evening she has fled to "a star above the sunset lees," and the
poet, unaffected by all this horror and strangely passive, is left to

> Gaze pensively upon the way she went,
> Drink at her font, and smile as one content. (p. 20)

This last line is important: the poet is not contented with his
vision, just as Fancy remained "unsatisfied" with all of the scenes
she visited. In a sense, then, the poem has evoked an ideal of
experience at the same time that it indicates the limitations of
that ideal. In search of beauty one must explore all possible
extremes of sensation, including horror. However, this is self-
defeating, because beauty is unattainable in any of its forms
and because an exploration of sensations for their own sake
can lead only to a kind of jaded voyeurism.

"A Wine of Wizardry" seems to spring from a typically
Decadent impulse to break free from the self into a fantasy
world, vaguely mystical but admittedly illusory: and impulse
reminiscent of Baudelaire but lacking Baudelaire's sense of
self-immolation. In a sense, the poem is incantatory, attempting
through language and imagery to create extremes of sensation,
and thus to release the imprisoned self from ordinary experience.
The dominant tone is of horror tinged with morbid fascination
and, occasionally, with macabre humor. But at the same time
there is a strange detachment throughout the poem, and its final
impression is jaded, disappointed, and *ennuyé*.

Like "The Testimony of the Suns," then, "A Wine of Wizardry"
is about the failure of transcendence and the need to escape
from the here and now. In "Testimony," the infinite abysses
of space provide a direction for imaginative escape, whereas in
"Wine" to escape is to retreat into fantasy. Both poems imply
the futility of human aspirations, and in both there is an under-

tone of hysteria which suggests the urgency of the problem
that ordinary reality will not solve. The poet's attempt to break
through the prison of self will always fail, and he will either be
left to ponder on oblivion—"dust the yearning lips that cried"[3]—
or to simulate pleasure—"smile as one content".[4]

This attempt to transcend the senses finds expression in several
of the shorter lyrics collected in *A Wine of Wizardry and Other
Poems*.[5] In "The Islands of the Blest," for instance, we see the
impulse to abandon external reality for the visionary as quickly
as possible:

> In Carmel pines the summer wind
>   Sings like a distant sea.
> O harps of green, your murmurs find
>   An echoing chord in me! (p, 21)

The wind in the pines quickly gives way to the movement of the
spirit; the nearby ocean is forgotten, and in its place is "a distant
sea" of metaphor, corresponding in turn to a spirit-sea within
the poet—a sea which may contain distant islands:

> Sometimes from ocean dusks I seem
>   To glimpse their crystal walls,
> Dim jewels of mirage that gleam
>   In twilight's western halls. (p. 22)

He has scented the fragrance of the isles in the sea air, and even
though no one will ever see them, and seamen would scorn his
story, yet the "Chart of Dreams, unrolled,/Attests their heaven's
jasper bourns,/Their reefs of sunken gold" (p. 22). The dream-
islands are yet another symbol for the ineffable but quite vague
ideal that may wait beyond the veil of consciousness. The arts
can give us hints of its existence, but cannot penetrate the veil.

In "Romance," another tribute to the poetic imagination,
Sterling employs a different tone, but uses a similar image of
a haven far beyond the spirit-sea. Departed Romance is personified as a crusading king who has returned to his home:

> Would that we might follow thy returning wings,
>   And in thy farthest haven beach our prow—

> Thy dragons conquered and thine oceans crossed—
> And find thee standing on the dust of kings,
>   A lion at thy side, and on thy brow
>   The light of sunsets wonderful and lost! (p. 30)

The grandiose quality of this poem is repeated in another, a tribute to Edgar Allan Poe, personified as a sort of seraph whose glories will outlast the achievements of kings. The visionary journey here is into the vague splendors of futurity, as in "Romance" and "Islands of the Blest" it was into the equally vague "havens" beyond the sea of consciousness:

> Time, who but jests with sword and sovereignty,
>   Confirming these as phantoms in his gloom
>   Or bubbles that his arid hours consume,
> Shall mold an undeparting light of thee—
> A star whereby futurity shall see
>   How Song's eventual majesties illume,
> Beyond Augustan pomp or battle-doom,
>   Her annals of abiding heraldry. (p. 28)

This motif of self-transcendence into vague realms, with its many versions in Sterling's poems, calls to mind Edward Engelberg's comment on Baudelaire: "In this deep forest of symbols [of Baudelaire's "Correspondences"] are all the world's contraries: innocence and corruption, good and evil, beauty and horror. In spite of their apparent fleetingness, scents and fragrances possess a kind of dialectical permanence; amber, myrrh, and frankincense bring to life an ecstatic and rapturous world that shadows forth a universe of magical and wondrous illusions. In this somnabulistic state man achieves correspondence with the world, not a world of objects but of smells and sounds, sights and touch."[6] Sensations, abstracted from the perceptions that generate them, become suggestions of an illusory world that lies somewhere beyond. The imagination, dwelling within this magical interplay of abstract sensations and their illusionary spiritual source, generates images which themselves create a new interplay between sensation and illusion. In the nature poem "An April Morning," for example, Sterling establishes correspondences between the beauty of Nature and the far more seductive beauty of Illusion. The spring morning is sensuous:

> Slow to the wanton sun's desire
> The vestal-bosomed buds unfold,
> Till poppies flaunt a silken fire,
> And buttercups a glassy gold.

Yet more appealing to the poet is the lure of the unreal:

> Till half I turn to hear again
> The flutes of Arcady at dawn,
> And rout of hurrying nymphs that feign
> To dread the kisses of dawn. (p. 66)

Like so many other Decadent poems, "An April Morning" displays a flight from the real into the unreal, from the natural into the imaginary. Furthermore, there is a kind of dialectic between the sensuousness of nature and the seductiveness of the imaginary nymphs. But there are two qualities that mark the limits of Sterling's flight. First, the language that he uses to portray his impression of this imaginary realm is drawn from the stockpile of imagery and allusion of the English Romantic poets. Thus it seems that Sterling is retreating into "bookishness" rather than into genuine visionary experience. Second, the movement itself is a "half-turning," one of a number of similarly tentative gestures in Sterling's poetry. There is no impulse to plunge madly into this dialectic of sensation and illusion; there is none of the immersion in the destructive element of mind which characterizes Baudelaire. So in two ways we must qualify the comparison between Sterling and the Symbolists like Baudelaire. Sterling is more a Decadent; and if we are tempted to see a Decadent as a poet of poses and tentative gestures, we still must be aware that in the Decadents, as in their predecessors the Symbolists, the lyric impulse stems from a desperate need to escape from the banality and meaninglessness of ordinary life, and a correspondingly desperate perception that the end of the escape may well be an abyss.

But we are not aware of desperation as we examine most of

the poems in *Wine*. We are, of course, aware of the dominance of the escape motif: into romance in "The Forest Mother," into the raptures of love in "The Lover Waits," into an ideal of art in "The Soul Prismatic," and into a naive celebration of nature in *The Triumph of Bohemia,* Sterling's first verse-drama.

This latter work, composed for the Bohemian Club annual revels, takes place in a grove of giant redwoods, where the Tree-Spirits are beset by various evil forces: the Spirit of the Four Winds, the Spirit of Time, the Spirit of Fire. They are victorious against all of these, but cannot withstand the axes of the Woodmen. Then the Spirit of Bohemia intervenes and converts the Woodmen to his service. All have agreed to make the grove a shrine for the worship of Bohemia, when arch villain Mammon appears, tempting with gold his former servants the Woodmen. But Bohemia slays Mammon, thus liberating the Tree-Spirits from all of their enemies. As entertainment for vacationing businessmen at a summer camping outing, this drama has certain unconscious ironies, and it also contains some rather flat lines ("Spirit of Fire: 'I come, whose hunger never yet had glut!' " [p. 106]). We see no foreshadowing here of the uses Sterling would make of the verse-drama form in his later career, but we do see a sort of carefree hedonism which is absent in most of his more serious compositions.

Nevertheless, there are a few poems in *Wine* in which Sterling more directly confronts the destructive implications of his flight from the real. In "A Mood," for instance, he uses the fatal woman figure which he would employ in later verse-dramas, in a rather masochistic romantic motif:

> I am grown weary of permitted things
>   And weary of the care-emburdened age—
>   Of any dusty love of priest and sage
> To which no memory of Arcadia clings;
>
> For subtly in my blood at evening sings
>   A madness of the faun—a choric rage
>   That makes all earth and sky seem but a cage
> In which the spirit pines with cheated wings.
>
> Rather by dusk for Lilith would I wait
>   And for a moment's rapture welcome death,

> Knowing that I had baffled Time and Fate,
> And feeling on my lips, that died with day
> As sense and soul were gathered to a breath,
> The immortal, deadly lips that kissing slay. (p. 73)

In the octave of this sonnet we see a double rebellion against the banal, everyday world of "permitted things." The sensuous nature, that subtle singing in the blood, wishes to rebel into a kind of "madness of the faun," for pure ecstasy of the senses. The spirit would be free also, and express its yearnings in a "choric rage." The fulfillment of both of these longings would be a moment with Lilith, and it does not matter that this would also be their final denial. Both body and spirit, "sense and soul" gathered together, would be snuffed in a single, ecstatic breath by Lilith's kiss. That ambivalent figure, then, is a symbol of ecstasy and agony, transcendence and despair—Sterling's Faustine.

This sonnet expresses more explicitly than most Sterling poems the motif of self-immolation in an instant's ecstasy which was the ultimate escape-fantasy of the Decadents. But another sonnet in *Wine* depicts a different sort of escape into death. "In Extremis" portrays a fearful storm at night, which in the octave evokes a host of characteristic images. The wind is like a war in heaven—like archangels in chariots, like high-blown trumpets mutinous and strong. But in the sestet—and this is very significant—the world of natural phenomena reasserts itself. The physical wind is too strong for the imagination to withdraw from nature into its own illusions. Thus, from the gaudy imagery of the octave (the visions invoked by the wind), the speaker is forced in the sestet to hear the wind's actual voice: "Till *louder* on the dark I heard/The shrieking of the tempest-tortured tree . . ." (p. 29; italics mine). This shrieking, and the deeper tumult of the nearby ocean, drown out the poetic mind. The resulting confrontation with wild nature itself might have led to a perception like that in Frost's "Storm Fear," in which the night storm itself becomes a metaphor for death and spiritual dissolution. But for Sterling a strange sort of avoidance attempts to neutralize rather than resolve the fearful confrontation:

But near the eternal Peace I lay, nor stirred,
Knowing the happy dead hear not at all. (p. 29)

Thus this storm is not like Frost's; instead, its stress is the
stress of the real overwhelming the imagined. The final reponse
is a more pronounced turning away from the real, not the
"half-turn" toward allusion and visionary images, but a sort of
shrinking of the spirit toward an enfolding, welcoming death.
Critics who condemned Sterling's "A Wine of Wizardry" by
asserting that he was avoiding life would find confirmation of
their views in this poem. But they would not have understood
the despair which prompts the reaction—the sense that something is terribly, desperately wrong with life itself.

A longer poem in *Wine*, "A Dream of Fear," uses a supernatural nightmare to present a vision of despair, much more
directly than the tentative gestures or the yearnings for oblivion
of the other poems in the collection. The poem's tone is quite
hysterical, but it also makes clear the "human implications" of
the philosophy Sterling espoused in "The Testimony of the
Suns." In fact, the use of the *In Memoriam* stanza form—to
my knowledge, the last time in his career Sterling used the
form—might lead us to speculate that "A Dream of Fear" is a
version of the second part of the earlier poem, as Sterling might
have written it without Bierce's damaging advice to retain the
"cosmic perspective."

There are two steps in the tonal movement of this long lyric,
from the irrational terror of the unknown to the terrors of
knowledge. The poem's first dream vision is a city of the dead,
a place actually *older* than death. Led by a ghostly hand, the
dreamer walks through this vast ruin, where a "half-wasted"
moon illuminates tombs in which time itself has died, or so it
seems. The unsettling fear of the scene gives way to a sort of
paranoia, when the night itself goes mad and messages run
from sky to tomb, indecipherable except to the dead. Yet the
speaker seems aware that this profane secret is a curse to the
living.

The poem shifts to a vision of the night skies, where the
meaning of this malignancy becomes clearer. The cryptic message is the "menace of infinity," the eternal curse that time-

lessness has made to time—the death knell of all life and all temporality in the face of an inhuman, infinite cycle of unliving stars—"Python's intolerable hiss/Told from the jaws of his abyss" (p. 80). Thus Sterling invokes the nebular hypothesis of "The Testimony of the Suns," but as a malignancy in the cosmos which is far from sublime. The terror evoked by this revelation is only intensified by the ending, when, summoned by some horrible law of recurrence, the dead awake:

> I saw the light of dreadful lanes,
> I heard enormous valves resound,
> For eons sealed in crypts profound,
> And clangor of ascending chains. (p. 81)

In this inversion of the Christian resurrection, Sterling attempts to express the despair of one who grasps the ultimate terrors of cosmic law. Whatever horror emerges from those tombs to live again, it will not be human.

In its way, "A Dream of Fear" is an apocalyptic vision, something like Yeats's "Second Coming," except that the ghostly presences ascending to be born are not in the immediate but in the far distant future, beyond all that we project of human life and all that we can comprehend as measurable time. Thus, within the melodramatic conventions of a supernatural poem, Sterling expresses his own particular type of alienation.

The three lyrics which we have just examined show more directly than elsewhere in the early poems the desperation which underlies Sterling's pessimism. They also show a rather ambivalent attitude toward death. Death is a transcendent rapture, as in "A Mood"; an anodyne for despair, as in "In Extremis"; or it is an occasion for metaphysical terror, as in "A Dream of Fear." With this ambiguous treatment of death, and the other dominant characteristics of the verse in *Wine*— the escape from the real into the visionary, the exotic, highly rhetorical language, the frantic straining after sensation, and the sense of an underlying abyss, we see how closely Sterling approaches the post-Romantic tradition of the English Decadence.

II *Sonnets of Sea and Stars*

Within a two- or three-year span following the appearance
of the notorious "A Wine of Wizardry" in Bierce's *Cosmopolitan,*
Sterling began to find an increasingly favorable reception in the
national literary magazines, and significantly, it was with the
sonnet form that he found his most appreciative public. At this
time the sonnet was very popular both with critics and general
readers of poetry, and Sterling's excursions into the form began
to be highly regarded.

The sonnet form allowed Sterling to develop some of the
restraint he needed to counter his tendencies toward extrava-
gance and bombast. The sonnet's brevity and the discipline
enforced by its metrical pattern helped him to avoid the diffuseness of the longer poems, and allowed him to exploit
sound-values without drowning his music in a deluge of imagery
and allusion. Even the most grandiose of his conceptions show
to better advantage:

Oblivion

Her eyes have seen the monoliths of kings
    Upcast like foam of the effacing tide;
    She has beheld the desert stars deride
The monuments of Power's imaginings.
About their base the wind Assyrian flings
    The dust that throned the satrap in his pride,
    Cambyses and the Memphian pomps abide
As in the flame the moth's presumptious wings.
There gleams no glory that her hand shall spare,
    Nor any sun whose rays shall cross her night,
        Whose realm enfolds man's empire and its end.
No armor of renown her sword shall dare
    No council of the gods withstand her might.
        Stricken at last Time's lonely Titans bend.[7]

The above is the first in a group entitled "Three Sonnets of
Oblivion." The second, "The Dust Dethroned," is similar, em-
ploying a series of allusions to past splendors which have
vanished. If we cannot agree with Alfred Kreymborg that the

poem compares well with Shelley's "Ozymandias,"[8] we might
still notice the starkly arresting qualities of such images as
"the lichens cling the closer with the years,/And seal the eyelids
of the weary god" (p. 146) and "The vulture shadows with
arrested wings/The indecipherable boasts of kings" (p. 146).
In the third sonnet of the group, "The Night of Gods," there is
a fine tercet,

> I stand as one whose feet at noontide gain
> A lonely shore; who feels his soul set free,
> And hears the blind sea chanting to the sun. (p. 147)

"Three Sonnets of Oblivion," the first of Sterling's poems to
reach a major literary periodical, appeared in the *Century* of
September 1908. From this time on, his sonnets appeared with
frequency in the magazines, and by the publication of *The House
of Orchids and Other Poems*[9] in 1911, he had published more
than forty.

In this third book of poems Sterling collected several other
sonnet groups similar to the "Oblivion" sequence: "Three Sonnets of the Night Skies," "Sonnets on the Sea's Voice," and
"Sonnets by the Night Sea." Their consistent use of ocean and
star imagery contributes to the overall tone of the volume, of
which one reviewer commented, "The best [poem] seems to
have been inspired by the solemn and sobering eternity of the
ocean."[10] In "Sonnets on the Sea's Voice," for instance, Sterling
employs several variations on the ocean's moods. The first
sonnet of the group contrasts the sea as man's symbol of eternity
with the true eternity which will silence the sea, long after
human life has ceased. In another, the sea's voice awakens the
speaker to the past: "I stand/With armies round about, and in
mine ears/The roar of harps reborn from legend's dust" (p. 41).
And the best sonnet of the sequence contrasts the attraction of
a forest glade and its single iris, an emblem of Faith, with the
wild, Satanic desire to be on the tempestuous seas at midnight,

> Where the wind's unreturning charioteers
> Lash, with the hurtling scourges of the sea,
> Their frantic steeds to some tempestuous goal—
> The deep's enormous music in their ears. (p. 42)

Again the stars and the ocean are vehicles for lofty meditation on the meaning of human existence in the "Sonnets by the
Night Sea." The measured cadence of the ground-swell, in the
first of the group, suggests to the speaker the meaningless pro-
gression of the soul, "Swung as a pendulum from life to sleep,/
From sleep to life, from Timelessness to Time" (p. 117). The
deep itself speaks the eternal mystery in another:

> So blinded powers from their darkness seek,
> Thro human sight, that secret to attain?
> From fonts how distant is the spirit fed? (p. 118)

"Three Sonnets of the Night Skies" employ the same setting,
the starlit sky above the ocean. But in this group, instead of
metaphysical speculations, the poems are impressionistic mood
studies. "Aldebaran at Dusk," for example, portrays the pure
beauty of the evening. Sterling employs several precious but
effective rhythmical variations and patterns of assonance and
alliteration within the scheme of the sonnet, and succeeds in
generating a graceful fusion of imagery and sound:

> Thou art the star for whom all evening waits—
>   O star of peace, come tenderly and soon,
>   Nor heed the drowsy and enchanted moon,
> Who dreams in silver at the eastern gates
> Ere yet she brim with light the blue estates
>   Abandoned by the eagles of the noon.
> But shine thou swiftly on the darkling dune
> And woodlands where the twilight hesitates.
> Above that wide and ruby lake to-West,
>   Wherein the sunset waits reluctantly,
>   Stir silently the purple wings of Night.
> She stands afar, upholding to her breast,
>   As mighty murmurs reach her from the sea,
>   Thy lone and everlasting rose of light. (p. 22)

The other two sonnets of this sequence are not so effective.
"The Chariots of Dawn" personifies the morning star as a
"great captain of the dawn." Even in this poem, inspired by the
eastern sky, there are allusions to the sea: "Now am I minded

of some ocean-king/ . . . [who] passes down the seas to some strange doom" (p. 23). The artifice in the poem seems forced. So do the mythological allusions in "The Huntress of Stars," in which Artemis's horses and chariot pause before beginning their assault on the constellations, whose "nebulous, phantasmal breath" (p. 24) mists the winter skies.

Aside from the sonnet groups, *The House of Orchids and Other Poems* contains a sonnet which eventually became Sterling's most consistently praised and most anthologized poem.

The Black Vulture

Aloof within the day's enormous dome,
 He holds unshared the silence of the sky.
 Far down his bleak, relentless eyes descry
The eagle's empire and the falcon's home—
Far down, the galleons of sunset roam;
 His hazards on the sea of morning lie;
 Serene, he hears the broken tempest sigh
Where cold sierras gleam like scattered foam.
And least of all he holds the human swarm—
 Unwitting now that envious men prepare
  To make their dream and its fulfillment one,
When, poised above the caldrons of the storm,
 Their hearts, contemptuous of death, shall dare
  His roads between the thunder and the sun. (p. 30)

This sonnet was popular in part because it was not, like most of Sterling's poems, disparaging of human progress; American poetry in 1911 was still very much in the service of Uplift. Furthermore, "The Black Vulture," with its reference to the airplane, is much more available than Sterling's more allusive and "classical" poems.

Looking at the sonnets that appeared in *The House of Orchids and Other Poems*, one can see that certain essential characteristics of Sterling's lyrics were unchanged by his growing inclination for the sonnet form. The nebular theme of "The Testimony of the Suns," the pervasive agnosticism, the persistent striving after the ineffable, the love of cold images of Beauty, and the lyric raptures remain. But the sonnet offers Sterling some control

over his most distressing tendencies: diffuseness of thought
and excesses of imagery, allusion, and rhetoric. In poems like
"Aldebaran at Dusk," the sonnet form permits him to exploit
his most promising lyric asset: a careful attention to verbal
effects, generating a mood of quiet beauty tinged with a strain
of melancholy.

By and large, Sterling was quite comfortable with the sonnet
form, and it was as a sonneteer that he began to develop his
widest reputation. He acquired the utmost facility in composing
them, remarking once to a friend that he had never taken over
forty minutes to compose one. On several occasions he amazed
his friends by producing a technically perfect sonnet in less
than ten minutes. He wrote scores, perhaps hundreds, of love-
sonnets for his amours of the moment. Although these were not
intended for publication, two collections appeared in book form
after his death—*Sonnets to Craig* (1928) and *Poems to Vera*
(1938).

The anecdote of Sterling's composition of *Sonnets to Craig*
has already been told (Chapter 2). By the time the book was
published, few critics remained who favored its traditionalism.
One reviewer remarked, "These 'Sonnets to Craig' are a tribute
of which any woman might well be proud her life long. But they
do not constitute great poetry . . . , they are essentially the
property of one person alone."[11] In truth, the poems are very
uneven, betraying their too-facile composition. Yet the best of
them are graceful expressions of thoroughly conventional sentiments:

> I, who was lonely Beauty's loner priest,
>   (If solitude of heart so testify)
>   Stand loneliest now, with all that heart a sigh.
> The music of the world has never ceased;
> Still bloom the dawn's wide lilies on the east
>   And still the faces of the gods go by,
>   But down at evening from the quiet sky,
> When spirits muse, dream-held and dream-
>   released.
> What sun has made Time's mystery a light,
>   Simple and splendid as the litten dew

> By day-warm grasses gathered from the night?
> What golden spell is on familiar things,
> That all seem marvelously strange and new,
> That sunset now seems thronged with
> heavenly wings?[12]

Lewis G. Sterner's *The Sonnet in American Literature* (1930) surveyed some 226 of Sterling's sonnets. These do not by any means comprise the complete body of sonnets Sterling wrote during his lifetime; yet Sterner's study ranks him fourth among American poets in the total number of sonnets. Like most of his contemporaries, Sterling wrote entirely in the Petrarchan form, using variation only in sestet rhymes. Sterner evaluates him as "high in the ranks of American sonneteers," with "workmanship beyond cavil,"[13] thus reflecting a critical opinion common during Sterling's own lifetime.

III *"The House of Orchids"*

The House of Orchids and Other Poems (1911),[14] Sterling's third volume, represents a milestone in his career for two reasons. First, it is with this collection that he became completely established with the American public as a significant poetic voice; no longer was he a poet of regional fame, but a promising younger poet. Second, and paradoxically, *House of Orchids* was the *last* volume of poems that Sterling could produce with such assurance. Ever after, as we shall see, he would have to cope with the awareness that his Decadent manner was out of fashion and that the wave of the future would be a *vers libre* which he could not hope to and would not wish to imitate. How these two perceptions can be simultaneously true is a peculiar irony of Sterling's career, and is also the key to his importance as a transitional figure in the history of American poetry.

With near unanimity, the reviewers of *House of Orchids* praised the groups of sonnets we have already discussed. Most of the other sonnets within the collection reflect Sterling's obsession with fleeting beauty, change, and the ways of the poetic imagination. In "The Tides of Change," for instance, Beauty's presence in the world is seen as only an echo of the past or as a dim foreshadowing of some distant future. "The Sibyl of Dreams" and "The Music of Sleep" present dreaming as an intuitive process which can apprehend the phantom Beauty, a vision denied to the waking self. "Memory" presents the process of recollection as a faculty quite identical with the imagination. Memory is like a diver into the ocean of the past, and what she recovers is the "glory" that is unattainable to the present:

> Some shadow of the glory she restores,
>> Tho' wind and wave devour the ships of Dream;
>> For many mark her ere the fall of night,
> When the swift sound is mighty on her shores,
>> Singing, as wildly on her bosom gleam
>> The sea-dews, and the rubies of the light. (p. 28)

In these, as in so many of his poems, we see Sterling's great debt to Shelley and Keats.

Adopting the more grandiose style of poems like "Ozymandias," Sterling exploits once again in "The Moth of Time" his cosmic theme. Man is a "vision of the dust," not the immortal being he pretends to be: "Whence all thy thirst for God, thy piteous lust/For life to be when matter's chain shall rust?" (p. 29). All of our hopes for justice in the laws of the universe are like mirages at the edge of the desert. In "The Forty-Third Chapter of Job," Sterling borrows the cadences of the King James Bible to make a similar statement. God questions Job: "To what end dost thou search me, seeing that my wisdom is not as thine?" He presents himself as both arbitrary and cruel, the lord "of strange laughter." Much like Twain's Satan in *The Mysterious Stranger,* this arrogant God delivers unequal justice, slaying princes in their youth but allowing slaves to grow old in their misery. He allows pain and sin to triumph over human happiness: "I shall bar thee from thy joy with a thread of gossamer; I shall bind thy sin to thy children's children with ropes of adamant." And finally, he reveals himself as the arbitrary principle of cosmic law, who will make a "desolation" of earth, and a "quenched ember" of the moon. His message to Job and to mankind is degradation: "Be thou abased, for they are yet unborn that shall lay thee out; the worm is unhatched that shall consume thee. . . . Be thou bowed down, nor question the pains that I have set over thee: for each thing have I ordained its shadow" (pp. 137–40).

In an otherwise favorable review of *The House of Orchids,* the *New York Times* could find no praise for this poem: "Mr. Sterling has added to his earlier unusual qualities of imagination and of expression the restraint needed to make them truly effective. He invites anti-climax by placing 'the forty-third chapter of Job' last in the book; there seems to be no characterization wholly suitable to it save that of 'stunt.' "[15] Despite the reviewer's disapproval (which probably was prompted by a genteelist aversion to its blasphemy), the grandiosity of the poem does not seem as excessive as in others, and the allusions, drawn primarily from the Bible, acquire a decorum that is lacking elsewhere, when Sterling's "sublime" style falls into bombast. This latter tendency is exacerbated when the "sublime" lyric deals with nature.

Despite the continuous emphasis on universalism in the familiar cosmic themes, the nature poems in *House of Orchids* are distinctly regional. When, for instance, in a sonnet he employs the motif of sunset over the ocean—a favorite symbol for passing time, oblivion, or the inevitability of death—he is also reminding the reader that he is a West Coast poet. Biographical evidence indicates that Sterling was an excellent observer of the physical world. From his childhood on, as his friends have testified, he possessed a keen awareness of birds, wildflowers, and the beautiful minutiae of nature that the less observant would pass over. The five Carmel diaries, with their frequent descriptions of changing seasons, attest to his perceptive eye. Yet the poems in *House of Orchids* which are inspired by the northern California coast seldom portray nature accurately or objectively. Instead, like the earlier nature poems we have already examined, the observed setting serves as a point of departure into the subjective and visionary.

In "An Altar of the West," for example, an irregular ode of some 220 lines, the specific locale is Point Lobos, the southern boundary of Carmel Bay. But there is no sense of particularity in Sterling's portrayal of this spot; it could be any awesome headland or, for that matter, nearly any natural object which

gives the observer an impression of great beauty. In fact, the
first sixty lines are an extended apostrophe to Beauty, who
animates the "dryad-haunted" hills, and who inspires the
"ghostly rains" of the "wine-souled" autumn season. When at
last Point Lobos itself is mentioned, it is described in a rather
subjective and rhetorical manner:

> Past Carmel lies a headland that the deep—
> A Titan at his toil—
> Has graven with the measured surge and sweep
> Of waves that broke ten thousand years ago.
> Here winds assail
> That blow
> From unfamiliar skies
> And isolating waters of the West. (p. 67)

Point Lobos is a "vast, Tree-shaggy land," a "granite bulwark,"
a "mount of granite, steep and harsh, where cling/Along its
rugged length/The cypress legions" (p. 68). The poem makes
that familiar tentative movement from the real to the imagined:

> See how the wave in sudden anger flings
> White arms about a rock to drag it down!
> No siren sings,
> But in that pool of crystal gleams her crown,
> Flung on a rocky shelf—
> Grey jewels cold and agates of the elf
> That in yon scarlet cavern still is hid,
> 'Mid shells that mock the dawn. (pp. 69–70)

This ostentatious diction carries the poem through a long
afternoon, evening, and night at Point Lobos. Sterling's real
subjects, however, are the relation of human life to the universe
and the transitory nature of beauty. It is nature poetry like this
that prompted the Imagist critics to dub Sterling and Edward
Rowland Sill, an earlier poet, "The cosmic California school."[16]

Following the starry night to the moment when the abysmal
"writhing fog" comes to obliterate all the beauty of the shore-
line, "An Altar of the West" comments that Beauty has no
business haunting the House of Death. Though beauty seems a

portent of eternity, it may well be the "ray that leaping from our whitest star/Shows but the night beyond." Yet, in a now typical equivocation, Sterling speculates that beauty may be "The altar of an undiscovered shore," or the mad, sublime vision of "sorrowed man, the brute that dared to dream" (p. 75).

The objective world of nature is neglected equally in "The Gardens of the Sea," a lyric whose encrusted imagery nearly rivals that of "A Wine of Wizardry":

> Beneath the ocean's sapphire lid
>   We gazed far down, and who had dreamed,
>   Till pure and cold its treasures gleamed,
> What lucent jewels there lay hid?
> Opal and jacinth, orb and shell,
>   Calice and filament of jade,
>   And fonts of malachite inlaid
> With lotus and with asphodel, —
>
> Red sparks that give the dolphin pause. . . . (p. 86)

The colorful spectacle of the tide pools allows the poet's fancy to drift into ever more extravagant visions, with the ultimate mystical possibility that "the lilies of the moon" might appear beneath the sea. Clearly, the dominating impulse behind this lyric and others like it is the sheer love of decorative embellishment, but beneath the excesses of the rhetoric we sense a profound disappointment in the real.

A similar disappointment seems to dominate the title poem, "The House of Orchids." But where "The Gardens of the Sea" employs pure fantasy, this long lyric attempts to establish a relationship between natural objects and a half-remembered possible spiritual realm. But there is no vision of a timeless world beyond the senses—as there is in Keats, for example—and the poem seems at the end to retreat to the simple sensations with which it began.

The setting is a greenhouse into which the speaker has just stepped, as if to another land and another season. Outside "the day/Was cool with . . . breath of mounded hay/That ripens on the plains " But within, the fancy is awakened by the warm, moist air, "Warm as a Lesbian valley's afternoon." A mood is

created by this richly perfumed air, leading the mind to a vision
of "rainbow-haunted lands beyond the sea/And ocean-ending
sands" (p. 31).

The flowers themselves seem impossible, creations of an
almost supernatural order:

> Till now I did not deem
> That Beauty's flaming hands could shape in bloom
> So marvelous and delicate designs. (p. 32)

In fact, the orchids are like "exiles" from a divine realm of pure
Beauty, "more beautiful because they die so soon/ . . . Less of
the form than of the soul of things" (p. 33). It is especially
poignant that these blossoms should have such a fleeting existence, yet be so close to pure and timeless Beauty. Sterling
borrows from Wordsworth:

>   . . . ye
> Seem spirit-flowers born to startle man
> With intimations of eternity
> And hint of what the flowers of Heaven may be. (p. 33)

But these "intimations of eternity" only emphasize how man
is cut off from any hope for the eternal, and the beauty of the
flowers becomes a correlative for the melancholy of the poet,
who is now newly aware that his own life is as transitory as
theirs. Moving from orchid to orchid, he imagines scenes of
impossible loveliness, associated with the special qualities of
each flower. One, "wan and mystical," reminds him of "spirits
of the dew/That weep at silvern twilights silently." Another
would be more appropriate "In purple grottos where the stain-
less sea/On sands inviolable swirls." And the whiteness of
another evokes melancholy images of "palace-glooms where
queens have wept" (p. 35). The moment moves finally to a
sense of the evanescence of life and the universality of regret:

> Ah! they too slept at last,
> Whose sighs are half the music of the Past!

But here (line 83), in a new verse paragraph, the poem shifts sharply in tone. Suddenly the orchids seem malignant, spawned of demonic rather than divine forces. Their tropical luxuriance suggests depravities, evil spells, and destructive passions:

> But thou, O palest one!
> Dost deem to scorn the sun,
> And, in a tropic, dense,
> Languid magnificence,
> Desire to know thy former place,
> Where no man comes at night,
> And in its antic flight
> Behold the vampire-bat veer off from thee. . . . (pp. 35–36)

Now the visions evoked by these sinister plants include "goblin's eyes," "baleful rubies," and a flower that seems like a "mottled moth of Hell." Even the most beautiful of the orchids seems to reveal an underface of evil: "Witch-blown thou seem'st to be,/ For Lilith would have bound thee in her hair." A pale orchid with a crimson center

> . . . gleams
> Red as Adonis' wound it seems
> By Syria mourned of old,
> Or scarlet lips that drink from bowls of jade,
> Slowly, an ivory poison, sweet and cold. . . . (p. 38)

It seems that the imagination of the perceiver has become infected, so that he envisions only evil. Or it might be that he has moved from the appearance of beauty to a subtler reality of evil. This second speculation is supported by the beginning of the last verse paragraph:

> Oh! mystically strange
> That speechless things should so have power to hint,
> With subtle form and tint
> That seize the heart's high memories unaware,
> The sorrow and the mystery of Change,
> And elements in Fate's controlling plan
> Not altogether ministrant to man
> Nor mindful of his care— (p. 38)

The evanescent beauty of the orchids, then, represents change; their opposing poisonous attraction, despair. Both are the "heart's high memories"—another allusion to Wordsworth—and both are aspects of Sterling's pessimism. In the duality of these orchids we see an early statement of the "pleasure and pain" metaphysic of Sterling's later years: beauty and pleasure are fleeting; pain is lingering, and relievable only by the oblivion of death. In the face of these harsh truths, the spirit either longs for an impossible purity and immortality, or madly searches for destructive extremes of sensation:

> Some joy to death akin,
> Or tragic kiss, or fruit malignly fair,
> Some garden built by sin
> For Love to wander in. . . . (p. 38)

In the progress of the meditation, the physical orchids have served only as a vehicle for the speaker's imaginative flights. Yet suddenly, in the last twelve lines, he reminds himself of the purity and innocence of the flowers themselves, implying that the malaise of the preceding 140 lines is the fault of the perceiver, not of mute flowers:

> And yet, O blossoms pure!
> How marvelous the lure
> Of your fragility and innocence—
> This grace and wistfulness of helpless things
> That ask no recompence!
> Ye give the spirit wings,
> For yours the beauty that is near to pain
> And stir the heart again
> With visions of the Flowers that abide—
> Ah! sweet
> As when love's glances meet
> Across the music, heard at eventide! (pp. 38–39)

Often in Sterling's poems the ending softens the dominant cynicism of the rest of the work. There is evidence that he deliberately tried to spare his readers from the more despairing side of his vision, by tacking on endings that he did not really endorse; the practice might also have been an attempt to meet the overgenteel requirements of his magazine publishers, requirements which, despite himself, influenced him. But in the final analysis this sort of equivocation must be seen as a reluctance to confront the implications of his own pessimism, which threatened the foundation on which his lyrical impulse was so precariously poised.

CHAPTER 5

The Disease of Art

As We have documented in the biographical chapters, the years surrounding World War I were a time of intense personal crisis for Sterling. There were several contributing factors: his alienation from Bierce and the latter's disappearance into Mexico, his divorce, Jack London's death, his ex-wife's suicide. Here, however, we will examine yet another aspect of the crisis: the impact of the American "poetic renaissance" on Sterling's rigidly defined aesthetics. The ways in which he tried to compromise—even to efface—his own assumptions about art in adapting to the changing demands of his audience will be the concern of this chapter.

I *The Browning Ode*

In the same year that Sterling moved to Carmel, the Harvard poet George Cabot Lodge had written of the cultural trap in which he and his contemporaries had found themselves that "the whole core of the struggle, for ourselves and for our art, is to emerge from the envelope of thoughts and deeds which are not our own, but the laws and conventions and traditions formed of a kind of composite of other men's ideas and emotions and prejudices."[1] The poets of Lodge's generation, except for Robinson, did not find a way to escape this "envelope" of the derivative; yet by 1911 a new era in American poetry was imminent: it was the eve of the Imagist rebellion.

Eliot had written but had not yet published "The Love Song of J. Alfred Prufrock." Stevens, Frost, Williams, Hilda Doolittle, Marianne Moore, and Richard Aldington were quietly at work. Pound, the prime mover of them all, was in London, and *Personae* had appeared in 1909. (Sterling had read in manuscript

112

"Ballad of the Goodly Fere" without noticing its brilliance; yet, curiously, Bierce did.) And among younger poets who were known to the public, there was a spirit of rebellion, a new rambunctiousness, a "barbaric yawp" of challenge which, however, Sterling saw as a manifestation of poetry's general decline. When the conservative Boston critic William Stanley Braithwaite commissioned him to write a poem for a Browning symposium, Sterling wrote an ode which makes the last point quite explicitly. Focusing on the relationship between Browning's sensibility and his own, Sterling affirms that his true ties are with the past.

The ode begins by stressing Sterling's former inability to appreciate Browning's concern with suffering humanity:

> Nor would I hear
> With thee, superb and clear
> The indomitable laughter of the race;
> Nor would I face
> Clear Truth, with her cold agates of the well,
>
> Nor with thee trace
> Her footprints passing upward to the snows,
> But sought a phantom rose
> And islands where the ghastly siren sings.[2]

Here Sterling seems to be acknowledging that his own devotion to Beauty is an illusory dedication, and in the face of Browning's integrity to see things as they are, his own is a paltry sort of achievement.

The poem continues with a hyperbolic tribute to Browning's greatness. He is a warden against "the dragons of man's ancient fear," a leader among the few who hear "the music of God's silence" (here Sterling seems to be ignoring Browning's assertive Christianity). Invoking a favorite image of the poet as a Superman, Sterling compares him to an eagle above the "wingless things of earth," and to a "voyager of seas within the cosmic solitude." Unlike the lyric poets, Browning is not interested in

> The feigned passion of the nightingale
> Nor shards of haliotis, nor the song

> Of cymballed fountains hidden in the dale,
> Nor gardens where the feet of Fragrance
>   steal. . . . (p. 168)

Instead, Browning is privy to the "eternal undertone" at the
very heart of Nature. He is able to sense "The rainbows hidden
in the frustrate slime," the basic dignity of the world's pain, the
true beauty at the center of sordid humanity.

Accordingly, Browning's satirical mode is a sort of cosmic
laughter: "Yet hadst thou sharper strains,/ . . . Loosing the
sweet/High thunder of thy Jovian laugh/On souls purblind in
their self-righteousness" (p. 170). He is able to accommodate
in his mind the dialectic of baseness and grandeur in man; in
the best lines of the ode, Sterling praises Browning's breadth
of vision:

> And thou didst know what meat
>   Was torn to give us milk,
> What countless worms made possible the silk
>   That robes the mind, what plan
> Drew as a bubble from old infamies
>   And fen-pools of the past
> The shy and many-colored soul of man. (pp. 170–71)

In its final lines, the ode moves to a comparison between
Browning and the poets of the present day, who refuse to face
the dual nature of things. Some, the Decadents, turn futilitarian
and prophesy the end of civilization; some, the Socialists, prattle
of human brotherhood; and worst of all, the genteel Uplift poets
celebrate the status quo by masking their own spiritual bondage
and their loss of idealism in effete lyricism. As a Decadent, then,
Sterling is proclaiming himself far inferior to the Titanic Browning; and yet it seems that he is establishing his allegiance with
the older poet in the face of a general cultural decline. The
poem ends very conventionally with the hope that the present
generation may yet earn a more favorable place in the struggle
for human progress, with Browning as its inspiration.

When the "Ode on the Centenary of the Birth of Robert
Browning" appeared in the *Boston Transcript* on May 4, 1912,

it was very favorably received. Many poets wrote to Sterling praising it, and when in 1912 Mitchell Kennerley requested a poem for his *Lyric Year* contest, Sterling sent him the ode. This *Lyric Year* anthology itself marks a significant episode in the emergence of the modern movement in American poetry. A remarkably diverse mixture of poems appears within its pages, and there is an exuberance and a spirit of novelty that certainly is not typical of the previous few decades. The only widely known poem in the anthology, however, is "Renascence," submitted by Radcliffe sophomore Edna St. Vincent Millay. But traditionalism triumphed in the judging: the uplifting "Second Avenue," by Orrick Johns, won the first prize, and Sterling's conservative ode was second.

As the Browning ode attests, Sterling had clearly cast his lot with the nineteenth century, with a belief in the overriding value of pure lyricism in poetry, and a sometimes contrasting view of the poet as a "vatic shadow cast athwart the stars" (p. 171), a sort of cultural and cosmic prophet. And despite his praise of Browning, Sterling would not understand the importance of that poet to the modernist movement—the irregular, strong verses, the dramatic irony of the monologues, the use of masks. He would not completely comprehend the continuity between these achievements of Browning and the more radical poetics of Pound, Eliot, and Yeats. In 1913 Sterling wrote a sonnet entitled "The Coming Singer," which expresses his hope for a new major poetic voice, but which also dramatizes how far his conception of the poet's godlike role diverges from the actual achievements of Frost or Stevens.

> The Veil before the mystery of things
>   Shall stir for him with iris and with light;
>   Chaos shall have no terror in his sight
> Nor earth a bond to chafe his urgent wings;
> With sandals beaten from the crowns of kings
>   Shall he tread down the altars of their night,
>   And stand with silence on her breathless height,
> To hear what song the star of morning sings.
>
> With perished beauty in his hands as clay,
>   Shall he restore futurity its dream.

> Behold! his feet shall take a heavenly way
> Of choric silver and of chanting fire,
> Till in his hands unshapen planets gleam,
> 'Mid murmurs from the Lion and the Lyre.[3]

II *"Beyond the Breakers"*

Despite the critical success of *The House of Orchids and Other Poems*, and despite his now-secure reputation as a sonneteer of great skill, by 1913 it had become clear to Sterling that the magazines were not altogether receptive to his best work. They wanted "human interest" rather than chill aestheticism, direct expression of sentiment rather than recondite astronomical allusions or densely textured imagery. He was able to rationalize their criticism as the pedestrianism of the cultural Philistine, but when younger poets whom he respected concurred, he was forced to reevaluate his position. For example, in a newspaper interview in September 1912 Witter Bynner had remarked wittily that Sterling's poetry was "too stellar" and that it gave him "cosmic indigestion." He went on to say that he preferred Sterling's lighter vein to his more pretentious work.[4]

Opinions like this held some sway over Sterling, and when in 1913 he began consciously to try to make a living through his poetry he began to write lighter verse, more "human" in sentiment, and far less esoteric in diction or allusion. To some degree he was successful, but to the detriment of his own aesthetic views: art was anathema to the publishing world, and if he had to adapt himself to its standards, then he would have to get "the disease of art" out of his system.

The fourth collected volume, *Beyond the Breakers and Other Poems* (1914), attests to Sterling's resolve to write poetry that would please his critics—and to the difficulty he had in doing so. There are several set-pieces in Sterling's usual vein; for example, the sonnet "The Muse of the Incommunicable" presents a typical theme of the intransigence of beauty:

> The wind of lonely places is her wine.
> Still she eludes us, hidden, husht and fleet,
> A star withdrawn, a music in the gloom.

> Beauty and death her speechless lips assign,
> Where silence is, and where the surf-loud feet
> Of armies wander on the sands of doom.[5]

Other poems reflect customary concerns, and emphasize the deepening cynicism we have noticed in the previous volumes. "The Last Monster" describes man as the bestial product of centuries of bestial evolution. "War" and "Christmas Under Arms" portray the folly and brutality of war. "The Thirst of Satan" combines the familiar nebular theory with a melodramatic image of brooding evil:

> In dream I saw the starry disarray
>   (That battle-dust of matter's endless war)
>   Astir with some huge passing, and afar
> Beheld the troubled constellations sway
> In winds of insurrection and dismay,
>   Till, from that magnitude whose ages are
>   But moments in the cycle of the star,
> There swept a shadow on our ghost of day—
> A shape that clutched the deviating earth
>   And checked its headlong flight and held it fast,
>   Draining the bitter oceans one by one.
> Then to the laughter of infernal mirth,
>   The ruined chalice droned athwart the Vast,
>   Hurled in the face of the offended sun. (p. 51)

But many of the poems in *Beyond the Breakers* depart from the usual themes. The title poem, for instance, is a tribute to the manly sport of swimming. "Ballad of Two Seas" and "Ballad of St. John of Nepomuk" are excursions into light narrative verse. "Past the Panes" ends in a genteel cliché, "O strange! that humble things should be/Of stature more than mountains are . . ." (p. 104). There are even conventionally pious lyrics with sentiments completely at odds with Sterling's own views. In "The Palette," for instance, the beauties of nature are part of God's plan:

> Unheard, unseen, the eternal Alchemist
> Wakes the colors that slumber deep in
>   their darks.

> O myriad hues! and each one true to its
> > tryst—
> The gold of Arcturus' breast and that of
> > the larks. (p. 78)

Several poems exploit the popular taste for sentimentality which Sterling, following Bierce's example, had always deplored. "Willy Pitcher," for instance, is a rather slender lyric about a dead childhood friend. A sighing, melancholy tone and highly conventional sentiment are its major characteristics:

> And yet across the years
> I see us roam among the apple-trees,
> Telling our tale of boyish hopes and fears
> Amid the hurried bees. . . .

> Till I am half content
> Not any more the loneliness to know
> Of him who died so young and innocent,
> And ah! so long ago.

It is especially poignant that the poet should be the only one who remembers the dead youth:

> Dead, and his kindred dead!
> And none remembers in that quiet place
> The slender form, the brown and faunlike head,
> The wildly wistful face. (pp. 65–66)

Variations of this particular motif—the wasted life—appear in several more fully personal lyrics. For example, in "The Man I Might Have Been" Sterling compares himself to the somewhat ruthless individual he might have become had he followed his uncle into the commercial world. And in "The Master-Mariner," he finds his own calling quite inferior to the more adventurous and virile life of his grandfather, a sea captain:

> My grandsire in his ample fist
> The long harpoon upheld to men:
> Behold obedient to my wrist
> A grey gull's-feather for my pen! . . .

> I think my grandsire now would turn
> A mild but speculative eye
> On me, my pen and its concern
> Then gaze again to sea—and sigh. (p. 16)

In "Beyond the Sunset" a similar statement is made. "Hard Ulysses," who traveled uncharted seas, must have been far braver than today's seamen. Again the heroic past is juxtaposed with the mundane present; mystery is gone from the world:

> But unto us the sea
> Lies sounded and familiar, and our rule
> Is over empires that the child at school
> Must learn by name, but which old Ulysses
> Held buried in his faith's wide mysteries. (p. 69)

A long-dead boyhood friend, a poet who longs for a world of action but who dreams away his life, these figures reflect Sterling's sense of the plight of contemporary man—trapped in the mundane, and equally trapped by his own dreams of escape. This perception is especially resonant if we compare it with similar statements by some of Sterling's contemporaries; we are reminded of Robinson's Tilbury Town nonentities, Masters's Spoon River dead, and Anderson's Winesburg grotesques, all caught in the backwash of their own illusions. Hence Sterling is expressing one of the major naturalistic themes of an emerging twentieth-century American literature.

In the sonnet "Omni Exuent in Mysterium" Sterling expresses the same sentiment in his usual poetic voice, rather than the lighter persona he adopts in some of the other poems. With this change in tone, the theme becomes a typical *fin-de-siècle* poetic statement of exalted unrest and pathos:

> The stranger in my gates—lo! that am I,
> And what my land of birth I do not know,
> Nor yet the hidden land to which I go.
> One may be lord of many ere he die,
> And tell of many sorrows in one sigh,
> But know himself he shall not, nor his woe,
> Nor to what sea the tears of wisdom flow,
> Nor why one star is taken from the sky.

> An urging is upon him evermore
>   And tho he bide, his soul is wanderer,
>   Scanning the shadows with a sense of haste
> Where fade the tracks of all who went before—
>   A dim and solitary traveller
>   On ways that end in evening and the waste. (p. 93)

Thus, even in the poems written to meet the demands of the public for sentimental and uplifting verse, Sterling could not abandon his pessimism.

Nevertheless, his efforts to write expressly for the market-place did meet with qualified success. "Willy Pitcher" and "The Master-Mariner" were widely admired and reprinted, and even more popular was the playful "Father Coyote":

> And father coyote waits no more,
> Knowing that down on the valley floor,
> In a sandy nook all cool and white,
> The rabbits play and the rabbits fight,
> Flopping, nimble, skurrying [sic],
> Careless now with the surge of Spring. . . .
> Furry lover, alack! alas!
> Skims your fate o'er the moonlit grass! (p. 132)

"Father Coyote" is one of several similar lyrics, collected in *Beyond the Breakers* under the faintly apologetic title "Natural History Items."

But another sort of nature poetry was more suited to Sterling's temperament and equally acceptable to the editors. When he exploited his gift for conveying quiet melancholy and abandoned the wild artificiality of earlier nature lyrics like "An Altar of the West," the result could be charming, as in "The Last Days":

> The bracken-rust is red on the hill;
> The pines stand brooding, somber and still;
> Grey are the cliffs, and the waters grey,
> Where the seagulls dip to the sea-born spray.
> Sad November, lady of rain,
> Sends the goose-wedge over again. (p. 130)

The dominant tone in this and in other lyrics of the California coast, like "Spring in Monterey," "The Mission Swallows," and "The Sleep of Birds," is a melancholy sense of fleeting, ever-elusive beauty. Impressionistic language helps to convey a combination of pathos and transcendent reverence:

> Linnet and gull, the dove and fluting thrush,
> Are silent in the reaccepted dark;
> The patient eagles drowse within the hush,
> And evening grasses hide the dreamless lark. (p. 126)

In this lyric we see that Sterling has abandoned his Decadent practice of using natural phenomena to invoke fanciful reveries which in turn embody affective or symbolic qualities. Instead, the perception of nature itself generates both the affective power and the thematic statement of the poem. The sadness of November is the sadness of all change.

But if the shift toward more "human" sentiment in Sterling's lyricism offered some promise in his nature poetry, and made his work more acceptable to conservative poetry editors, it certainly did not make him more palatable to the avant-garde who were now beginning to transform American poetry. Sterling's work was solicited for the early issues of *Poetry* magazine by Harriet Monroe, who felt that his poetry was "too fine for the popular magazines to appreciate."[6] Three poems appeared in the second issue of the magazine—"A Legend of the Dove," "At the Grand Canyon," and "Kindred." But before long *Poetry* was the recognized organ of the Chicago Renaissance and the chief American exponent of Imagism. And thus it is the central irony of Sterling's career that when he had at last in his forties established himself as an important younger poetic voice, the climate changed and he was regarded as middle-aged, passé, almost hopelessly out of date. It is a curious commentary on American literary history that a poet who seemed avant-garde in 1907, with the publication of "A Wine of Wizardry," should become an anachronism by 1916, when Harriet Monroe wrote that Sterling was prey to "the worst excesses of the Tennysonian tradition . . . , the frippery of a bygone fashion."[7]

III   *The Political Muse*

If anything, *The Caged Eagle and Other Poems* (1916) re-inforces the impression that Sterling's muse, beset by the double nemesis of genteel editors and Imagist critics, was in eclipse. Many of the poems betray their popular magazine destinations: "A Dog Waits His Dead Mistress," "An Autumn Thrush," "Time and Tear," "To an Old Nurse." Hackneyed and sentimental, these do not meet Sterling's own standards for serious work, but they had proven to be salesworthy.

Some of the poems in the volume have dignity, and one, "Conspiracy," is an effective Impressionistic lyric. Like de la Mare's "The Listeners," it involves the motif of the listening dead. The speaker enters in a vision a house of death, thinking as he knocks that a "cryptic murmur" has just ceased:

> Arctic, immense, no pillar stayed that hall,
> And from the north the melancholy light
> Sank through translucent windows, vast and white,
> On alabaster niche and frozen pall.[8]

He feels a chill presence in the crypt, and fears the "wisdom" of the corpses that lie rigidly on the marble slabs lining the white room. Afraid, he leaves the place:

> Whereat I turned, importunate, to win
> My way to life's complacencies once more;
> Which done, behind the safety of that door
> Again I heard that muttering begin.[9]

Despite the unsettling effect of "Conspiracy" and the occasional felicitous passages scattered through the volume, *The Caged Eagle* displays how far Sterling had moved from his own standards of art. Nevertheless, this volume contains two features of real interest to us: a series of occasional poems published for the Pan-American Pacific Exposition, and a sequence of short lyrics on the war in Europe. Both groups of poems are expressly political, and the pacificistic, socialistic tenor of the Exposition poems contrasts strangely with the chauvinism of the anti-German war verses.

As we have noted, by 1915 Sterling had long been a Socialist, but his political sympathies had largely been sequestered away from his work. Only occasionally had he allowed Socialist sentiments to appear in his verses, and, when they had, they were highly "idealized":

> In Babylon, high Babylon,
>> What gear is bought and sold?
> All merchandise beneath the sun
>> That bartered is for gold:
> Amber and oils from far beyond
>> The desert and the fen,
> And wines whereof our hearts are fond—
>> Yea! and the souls of men![10]

At times Sterling had written more directly on this theme of the corrosive effects of materialism on capitalist society. "In America," for example, is a diatribe against the misuse of wealth:

> Grown soft,
> Thy hands reach out for mercenary joys;
> Thy heart desires dishonorable loves
> And baser dreams. Yearly the golden chain
> Is weightier at thy wrists, and fostered pow'rs
> Plan in their dusk of tyranny thy tomb;
> And in that shadow Mammon's eyes grow fierce,
> And half thy sons adore him. Now the land
> Grows vile, and all thy statehood is a mart. . . .[11]

Yet Sterling, it seems, had rarely felt an impulse to write Socialist verse. He was so strongly opposed to didacticism of any sort in poetry that even the repeated appeals of his more politically active friends like Frederick Irons Bamford and Upton Sinclair were seldom heeded. Beset by many contradictions in his personal life—the relationships with Havens and with Bierce, for example—socialism had remained for Sterling little more than a sentimental political allegiance.

Hence it is surprising to see in *The Caged Eagle and Other Poems* so many verses with Socialist themes. In "Moloch," for instance, several stanzas present a dream-vision of an enormous,

hellish factory, which it seems should "surely" be operated by
giants and Titans. But in the last stanza, as the morning breaks,
the doors open, "And from those portals, black with smoke,/A
thousand weary children came!" (p. 69). And in a longer lyric
entitled "California," a tribute to the natural beauties of the
state ends with the sentiment:

> And thou art beautiful in all men's sight,
>   And all men laud thy ways,
> Who givest to the mercenary days
> A time and place for laughter and delight. (p. 83)

Likewise, the Exposition poems collected in the volume,
poems that more than any earlier work could be called verse-
for-hire, Sterling used very explicit Socialist themes. Perhaps
he was easing his conscience about the clearly occasional nature
of the poems, or perhaps the poverty which had plagued him
in New York City had made him more militant about injustice.
At any rate, in "The Builders," a lyric written to commemorate
the beginnings of San Francisco, Sterling praises both the de-
signers of the city and the greater heroes who will bring about
an end to war:

> A world reborn awaits us. Years to come
>   Shall know its grace and good,
>   When wars shall end in endless brotherhood,
> And birds shall build in cannon long since dumb.
> Men shall have peace, though then no man may know
> Who built this sunset city long ago. (p. 103)

"Yosemite: An Ode," separately published, contains an extended
and idealized description of the Yosemite Valley as it passes
from dawn through evening, and ends with an image of the
valley awaiting the true dawn of the human race:

> . . . waiting through the wistful years,
> The sure though distant tread
> Of those young armies of the Comrade State![12]

And finally in the lengthy "Ode on the Opening of the Panama-

Pacific International Exposition" Sterling made extended political statements which reflect neither his characteristic pessimism
nor his usual reluctance to compose didactic verse.

The "Exposition Ode" begins with a statement of the splendid
future that awaits California and, by quick extension, the human
race: despite the terrors of war, the reign of human friendship
and love is soon approaching. The first three sections are paeans
to man's progress through science, through art, and through
the careful husbandry of the land. Those forces in history which
have led to war and destruction have only engendered the de-
feat of the destroyers:

> And now the old betrayal of the dust
> Hath found them, striking from the anointed
> brow
> The crown, and sinking all the intrepid keels.
> The desert holds the oppressor and oppressed;
> The winds alone are great in Carthage now;
> The lizard and the lichen have the rest. . . . (pp. 94–95)

Why have all the demagogues of all ancient civilizations failed?
Sterling's answer is simple: "These are the realms that built on
self alone." And until the present, he continues, we have done
the same:

> For walked the Babylonian again
> Within our streets, once more should he behold
> The immeasurable Care,
> That ancient curse of poverty and gold, —
> The olden madness of division where
> The poor beg work, and beg for it in vain,
> And children slave, and stones are given
> for bread,
> While Mammon lolls on cushions of his fat,
> Whose glut not all the toils of men can sate. (p. 96)

The fourth section of the ode expresses fervently the hope that
this scheme of things may come to an end, that a "wiser age"
may bring a "fairer city" than now exists. And in the final part,
the vision of that "far city men shall build for Man" (p. 100)

elicits a lyric peroration proclaiming the end of the madness of ego, and the dawning of universal love.

These poems, so redolent of progressivism and of hope for a Socialist revolution which will end all war, are nearly unique in the body of Sterling's work. They certainly do not signal a permanent shift away from social pessimism, nor do they portend a movement away from the cosmic determinism of the earlier poems. By the early 1920s, as our examination of the verse-dramas will show, Sterling had become convinced that socialism would never redeem mankind from his pain. And in regard to the relation of art and social purpose, Sterling's long debate with Upton Sinclair, also in the early 1920s, illustrates his ultimate convictions in the matter.

Sinclair was writing *Mammonart* (1925), a Marxist indictment of the art world as a tool of the ruling class. His request for Sterling's reactions to the manuscript led to a series of long and impassioned letters. In one, Sterling remarked, "It's sure hell how you'll grab at straws to prove a point: As tho Poe wrote 'Ulalume' to give his ideas on immortality, or indeed for anything but that object so hateful to you, pure beauty untainted by propaganda." Further in the same letter Sterling refers to Tolstoy as a "great artist and befuddled prophet," remarking that "if he'd grasped my vision of the cosmos, he'd have gone crazy or, like Huysmans, entered a monastery."[13]

Yet during 1915 and 1916 Sterling's political muse was as active as it ever would be, and the optimism of his Exposition poems might arguably even be influenced by the Christian socialism of Tolstoy. And it seems clear that Sterling's confusion about his art and its potential for a public, reflected in the works discussed earlier in this chapter, is also apparent in the didacticism and the easy optimism of these poems. This impression of confusion increases as we examine the series of poems "On the Great War," included in the same volume with the pacifist works we have just discussed.

In Sterling's fourth volume, *Beyond the Breakers*, had appeared two pacifist poems, "Christmas Under Arms" and "War." In both, Sterling decries man's ceaseless lust for war and his tendency to make war a sort of mad, bloody religion. In "Christmas Under Arms" he raises the specter of imminent human extinction, and the question of the ultimate meaning of civilization, if it is only to be destroyed by man's bloodthirsty nature:

> Have we builded but for the flame, and sown that
> Death may reap?
> Shall we give our morning to murder and
> our noon to eternal sleep?[14]

There is no chance for humanity unless love and peace prevail: "Except the message be honored, a curse shall come to the lands/Where thou waitest on Christmas morning with a sheathless sword in thy hands!" Likewise, "War" displays much the same sentiment, but in a different form—a pair of allegorical visions. In the first, five Titans labor at a "red,/Infernal stithy." They feed their furnace with plows and hammers, then pound the molten product into an enormous sword. Their leader, a huge, bat-winged creature, seems loosely modeled after Milton's Satan, and the diction is somewhat Miltonic: "Two . . . poured a dangerous music on the dark,/With loud, astounding shock and counter-shock/Incessant. And the fifth colossus stood/The captain of that labor."[15] In the second vision, a mountain of houses, herds, and "all the handiwork of man" assails the eye. On the crest of the mountain are all valuable artifacts—gems, silks, and gold. Finally, all the fair sons of men are bound to this mountain, which becomes their pyre. As the smoke ascends from the infernal sacrifice, it takes the shape of the bat-winged master Titan of the first vision. When the pyre subsides and the baleful shadow diminishes, men make a second sacrifice to resurrect that war-god's shape.

The two poems show the excesses of Sterling's most grandiose manner, and probably in his own terms they are more propaganda than pure poetry. And though it may seem contradictory, there is no great distance from these pacifist poems to Sterling's war-verse of the next year; the rhetoric remains much the same, but the responsibility for the bloody rites of war and their human victims shifts—from mankind in general, to the "Hun"; from the baleful war-god, to the Kaiser.

The bloodthirsty lyrics which appear in *The Caged Eagle* and later in *The Binding of the Beast and Other War Verse* are distinctive in their hatred of all things German. Often they are in poor taste:

> Upon that charnel which thy hands have built
> Thy sword has graven all thy tale of guilt—
>   The names that Time shall sicken to recall.
>   Pollution is on thee like the mire
>   In which thine armies work thy dark desire
> And in whose slime thy sated princes crawl.[16]

Sometimes a gratuitous ircny combines with horror to produce a particularly unpleasant effect, as in the sestet of "The Little Farm":

> One laughed whom men had fettered to a tree.
>   Above his head a broken-hilted knife
>   Pinned a small hand that clasped a bit of string.
> And still he laughed, nor turned his gaze to see
>   The stripped and ravished body of his wife.
>   A weathered sign announced: No Trespassing.[17]

Yet, strangely, in some of the poems Sterling's worship of the heroic and grandiose interferes with his propaganda. "The Dream of Wilhelm II" seems to blend horror with unconscious admiration:

> He, a colossus towering toward the spheres,
>   With tyrant shadows casting triple night
>   On Europe, saw with dominating sight
> The great world-caldron seethe with futile
>   tears,
> And heard as with a god's commanding ears
>   The tread of armies whose resistless might
>   Should stay mankind's advancement to the
>   light,
>   But throne his dynasty a thousand years.[18]

Describing Wilhelm as a "colossus" in order to portray the tyrant's overweening pride actually involves the same language

and imagery that Sterling was wont to use in expressing the
sublime. This poem can be compared, for instance, with the
sestet of Sterling's "Chariots of Dawn," in which he writes of
the morning star:

> Now am I minded of some ocean-king
>   That in a war of gods has wielded arms,
> And still in slumber hears their harness ring
>   And dreams of isles where golden altars fume,
>   Till, mad for irretrievable alarms,
>   He passes down the seas to some strange doom.[19]

The paradox points to a contradiction—or at least an ambivalence—in Sterling's thinking. He admired the sublime forces in
the universe which were greater than the petty achievements of
men, and unconsciously he admired the overreachers who attempted to transcend human limitations. Hence the unwitting
overtone of hero-worship in his description of Wilhelm.

But, overall, the war poems are bitter music indeed, a testament to the strength of anti-German sentiment in the nation
as a whole, and, more directly, to the depth of Sterling's hatred.
A sonnet entitled "Germany in Belgium" proves the point:

> Mankind had dreamed its paltry dream of Hell,
>   And Satan gloating on a race undone.
>   Then through our mist of visions drove the Hun,
> And on the world a blacker shadow fell.
> So shall the fact deride, the truth dispel,
>   The flimsy web that childish minds have spun,
>   Till Horror bare her shambles to the sun,
> And that be told we whisper as we tell.
>
> God, when we pictured Hell, You must have smiled.
> Look down and see: abomination piled
>   Upon abomination! Flood on flood
>   Of tears outrung from innocence and age!
>   What spite of fiends is in the Teuton rage!
>   What visions of the Pit are in their blood![20]

When *The Binding of the Beast and Other War Verse* appeared

in late 1917, timed for the Christmas trade, it contained little
of the spirit of the season. The *Nation's* review of the book was
just: "Indignation is the last thing of which one should make
a business; Mr. Sterling undertakes to deliver it, in measured
qualities. . . . Too much drumfire either deadens or maddens,
and Mr. Sterling's verse is its literary counterpart."[21]

IV   Sails and Mirage

The publication of *The Binding of the Beast* was, aesthetically
speaking, probably the low point of Sterling's career, and it is
notable that after the war his confidence in his work seems to
have returned. He found a steady market for his poems among
more conservative literary journals; his poems appeared regu-
larly in *Nation, Bookman, Harper's Monthly, Literary Digest*,
and *Overland Monthly*. With this exposure he was rather widely
known, but primarily as a regional poet and a traditionalist.

The hated *vers libre* never tempted him; in fact, he inveighed
against it in print and even occasionally satirized it. For example, when approached in 1917 by Witter Bynner to join in
the famous *Spectra* hoax, a parody of Vorticism, he readily
assented. Under the pseudonym Yvonne Roux, Sterling contributed ribald "spontaneities":

> My aunt says she is
> Forty:
> She is
> Fifty-one.
> Once she was good-looking.
> She must have had
> Chances for many indiscretions.
> Now she hates modern
> poetry.
> And the audible amours of cats.
> Now she stands at the window,
> With her parched lips,
> And satin-backed hands,
> Hating our rooster and
> his successes.[22]

But Bynner decided not to use the contributions; somehow Sterling had missed the "vibrancy of ultimate fact" that Spectrism sought to capture. He could not effectively parody modern poetry because he despised it too much: to him it was simply illiterate. Some years after the *Spectra* incident, Sterling wrote his "formula" for modern verse: "take any thought of no importance, preferably one concerning one's own phases of nauseation, and state it as awkwardly and obscurely as possible. Voila! Cummings and Eliot!"[23] Clearly, Sterling did not understand the change in sensibility which generated Modernism; for better or worse, he was of the *fin-de siècle*. But in the 1920s, fortunately for him, there were many poets and critics who shared his views.

Sails and Mirage (1921), the last collected volume of new verse of Sterling's lifetime, is a testament to his acceptance of his own limitations, and his desire to make the best of them. Returning to the aestheticism of his earlier volumes, but dropping some of the archaisms and stilted diction which had weakened his style, Sterling produced his most consistently effective volume. Though essentially nostalgic in its adherence to the nineteenth-century tradition, *Sails and Mirage* contains some of Sterling's best poetry.

Aside from the disappearance of archaisms and poetic expletives ("Lo!" "Alas!") from this volume, several other characteristics of Sterling's work seem to have changed. Gone is the grandiose tone of voice which dominated "The Testimony of the Suns," the "Sonnets of Oblivion," and "The Binding of the Beast." For the most part, the bewildering phantasmagoria of imagery, as in "A Wine of Wizardry," is gone also. The tone is more restrained, less forced or strident. Devotion to beauty is still an important motif, but the vague Platonism and mystical speculation are completely absent, and in their place are poems which define Beauty as a life-sustaining illusion, and several poems which express longing for death. Thus the strain of pessimism, which we noted was growing in the first three volumes, dominates the last one.

Many poems are variations of earlier models. "The Setting of Antares," for example, is an impressionistic mood-piece quite like "Aldebaran at Dusk." In the octave of this poem, possibly

Sterling's best sonnet, there is a collection of images with complex tones. It is clear, and "the summer night is old"; there is a calmly moving sea, "with troubled moonlight on its tranquil breast." The wind and water have held a "truce of silence," and the stars are setting, "silvery and cold." Even with these conflicting connotations of age, grief, respite from strife, and beautiful, inhuman coldness, there is a feeling of unity in the scene, created by the tranquil cadences of the language, and by the resolution of the contraries, when the sestet shows us that the entire poem is about death:

> Antares, heart of blood, how stir your wings,
> Above the sea's mysterious murmurings!
>   The road of death leads outward to thy light,
>   And thou art symbol for a time of him
>   Whose fated star, companionless and dim,
>   Sinks to the wide horizon of the Night.[24]

Sterling also returns to earlier forms with three groups of ocean sonnets, two of which, "Sonnets by the Night Sea" and "Sonnets on the Sea's Voice," are continuations of sonnet sequences published in *The House of Orchids*. "Ocean Sunsets," a group of three linked sonnets, uses a unifying metaphor of sunset's journey around the world as a vast, endless billow of light which sweeps the oceans of the earth:

> Along the mighty rondure of the world
>   Forever and forever sweeps that wave,
>   From Arctic mountains to the southern floe,
> In soundlessness on purple islands hurled,
>   With opalescent wash of hues that lave
>   Old summits, sacred in that afterglow. (p. 13)

These sonnets, like many other poems in the volume, are pure mood-pieces—excursions into literary Impressionism, in which the emotional effect of the language is more important than its denotative content. An especially effective touch in the quotation above is the combination of "soundlessness," referring to the movement of light across the world, with the onomatopoeia of "opalescent wash," in which there is an impression of the sound of this "surf" of light. Thus Sterling plays delicately with the synaesthesia implied by his metaphor.

In the third "Ocean Sunsets" sonnet, Sterling abandons pure Impressionism to make a thematic statement which differs widely from similar earlier statements. Not only is Beauty—here, the beauty of sunsets—the fair ideal that we seek endlessly and fruitlessly, but it is our creation entirely. As long as there is a perceiving eye or a conceiving imagination, Beauty will exist. But when man is no more, Beauty will cease to be also:

> Thy marvel is of man and not of thee,
> And he being not, no longer shalt thou be.
> Parent and worshipper of loveliness,
>   He walks a realm forbidden to the brute.
>   An alchemist whose spirit can transmute
> Color and form to beauty's pure excess. (p. 15)

The solipsism of this statement represents Sterling's resolution of a long-term contradiction, which in fact is a central dilemma in all Decadent poetry. As a materialist he denied the existence of spirit, but as a poet the quest for spiritual beauty had been his primary inspiration. But here Beauty is understood as an act of the transforming imagination of man, not a vaguely Platonic ideal or a fleeting but transcendent Presence. Thus, in a way, Sterling is undercutting the principle by which he always has written poetry, exposing the false premises of his own notion of poetic inspiration, inherited from the Romantics but incompatible with materialism.

A similar idea dominates "Sonnets on the Sea's Voice." The sound of breaking waves, present for millennia, is "the ground-note of the planet's under-song." It has preceded and will succeed the life of man, and as such, it is completely alien to him. Yet some mysterious impulse within us would have us regard it as sublime music: "And what a mystery our hearts denote,/That hear from strands eternally unknown/The pulse of chords tremendous and remote?" (p. 115). In a "Sonnet by the Night Sea," the mournful wind dominates the night, but is silent by morning. Birds awaken when the wind's strength is

gone, but unlike the birds the speaker cannot forget its sound:
"With other tidings hast thou burdened me,/Whom desolations
harbor at the last" (p. 34). As always, Sterling avoids making
a completely personal statement.

In the nature poems of the volume, there is a similar avoidance of the personal. For Sterling, the speaker in the poem is
merely a medium for impressions; he would agree with Symons's
definition of the "ideal of the Decadence: to be a disembodied
voice, and yet the voice of a human soul."[25] For instance, in the
lyric "The Glass of Time," the only personal reference is in the
first lines, "I know a lake high up among the hills"; the rest of
the poem describes the beauty of the lake as a series of impressions and epiphanies, transmitted to the reader in an impersonal
but reverent tone. But at the end, the poem turns to the same
statement of the solipsism of beauty that we found in the ocean
sonnets:

> There if one comes, he fills that placid glass
>   With azure glory of the mirrored sky.
> Fading, the vision and the glory die
>   With him whose footsteps pass. . . . (p. 31)

Again, the beauty of the place would not exist without the
observer, and beauty's evanescence is the transitory nature
of man. In the final stanza, there is an apostrophe to the "Lake
of the spirit" which reflects the "pale mirage" of beauty as it
passes through our lives.

This "mirage" or illusion of beauty becomes the dominating
idea in several other nature poems in *Sails and Mirage*, most
notably "A Lost Garden," in which the presence of autumn in
the land is a "mournful" and "uncomforted" longing. But when
nature renews itself in spring, then the great deception will
recur. Sterling ends this poem in a series of contraries:

> Till Earth again confess
> Her dreaming heart has found
> The beautiful Illusion and its pain,
> So rich in happiness. (p. 29)

Thus the "rich happiness" of spring is an illusion which may only engender greater pain.

The gentle pessimism of the nature poems has its corollary in two personal lyrics, "The Passing of Bierce" and "Norman Boyer." In both of these poems Sterling defends suicide as an essentially fastidious act: "you turned in silence from the noise and light/To gain the soothing waste" (p. 70). In "Reason" Sterling defends the seeming pitilessness of that faculty which exposes the tawdry and the false. Yet in "The Wine of Illusion" the lie of transcendence is what sustains the spirit. A personified figure in "opalescent grey"—a color of illusions—stands surrounded by dead stars. She offers the speaker a crystal cup:

> "Drink this or perish. There is naught beside.
>   This is the draft that fashions men from swine,
>   And tho thy heart deny me in its pride,
> Yet of my cup of dreams its blood is red
>   And thy lips wet with my creative wine!" (p. 48)

The dead stars, of course, are symbols of man's transitory nature, and the wine, of the false ideals of beauty and immortality which have sustained him.

Testaments to the power of illusion, which supports life, and tributes to reason, which denies the value of life, these divergent expressions of Sterling's pessimism are the culmination of tendencies in his poems from the first. In the last ambitious works of his life, the verse-dramas *Lilith* and *Truth*, Sterling would integrate these divergencies into a consistent expression of despair.

CHAPTER 6

The Verse-Dramas

AMONG Sterling's best work are the three verse-dramas, *Lilith, Rosamund,* and *Truth*. Written late in his career, when he had learned to accept that his style and poetic subjects were out of fashion, they had little impact on the public. However, many other writers, including Dreiser, Mencken, Benjamin De Casseres, and James Branch Cabell, admired these poems exceedingly. Not only are they Sterling's most ambitious poems in terms of length, they contain philosophical themes more elaborately developed than in any of his earlier work. Together with the unpublished essay "Pleasure and Pain," the verse-dramas comprise the most complete articulation of Sterling's combination of Schopenhauerean pessimism, neo-Epicureanism, and cosmic nihilism. Further, they reflect the deepening despair that characterized Sterling's inner life during the years that led up to his suicide in 1926.

I Lilith

The allegorical *Lilith* (1920) is undoubtedly Sterling's best poem. It not only contains some of his most richly embellished verse, but it also has a carefully elaborated theme, implicit in shorter works but never fully developed until now. As mentioned earlier (Chapter 2), the idea for *Lilith* had occurred to Sterling as early as 1907. However, upheavals in his personal life and the need to make a living through occasional verse and short stories deterred him for years. If credit is due any other person for Sterling's completion of *Lilith*, it must be given to the poet John Neihardt, best known for *Black Elk Speaks* and his epic poem of the American West, *The Song of Hugh Glass*. Neihardt's encouragement during the most depressing years of

Sterling's life had a definite influence in preventing him from abandoning *Lilith* altogether. Like Sterling, Neihardt loved "costly, bejeweled, and richly tapestried" verse; also like Sterling, his own work was not in favor with the poets of the Chicago Renaissance. When he finished the poem, Sterling presented Neihardt the manuscript in gratitude.[1]

In the Cabala, Lilith was the first wife of Adam, who abandoned him and joined the demons, becoming the consort of Satan. Thus she is the principal demon in female form, mother of the succubi, snatcher of newborn infants, and sinful seductress *par excellence*. It is this last attribute of Lilith which made her a conventional figure in Decadent poetry and art. Alfred de Vigny interpreted her as "an impersonation of sensuality and sterility," who caused Cain to slay Abel, thus founding the religion of murderers. Dante Gabriel Rossetti praised her fatal beauty in poems and paintings. Remy de Gourmont drew upon Cabalistic traditions in his irreverent masterpiece *Lilith* (1891) and portrayed her as the seducer of Adam at the same time that Satan corrupted Eve. These are only a few of dozens of literary treatments of Lilith during the nineteenth century, nearly all of which treat her as a version of the archetypal *femme fatale*.

A beautiful seductress who brings both rapture and death, the *femme fatale* is a stock figure in late Romantic poetry. Swinburne's Faustine and Dolores, Keats's Belle Dame sans Merci, Gautier's Imperia, and Mérimée's Carmen all share an ambiguous combination of destructive sexuality and spiritual degradation. Some literary historians have considered the obsession with this figure as an expression of the *mal du siècle* of the late nineteenth century, and as a manifestation of the collapse of hereditary faith. Others, like Mario Praz, are interested in the *femme fatale* as a literary expression of the era's fascination with sexual perversity. Still other critics maintain that the interest in the *femme fatale* as a symbol of mingled pleasure and pain is a manifestation of the art-for-art's sake emphasis on pure sensation.

In Sterling's work, influenced as it was by the English Pre-Raphaelites and Decadents, the *femme fatale* appears frequently. He uses several versions of her in "A Wine of Wizardry"; many ballads contain beautiful witch figures, and his sonnets often portray a mood of longing for pleasure in pain, "the lips that kissing slay." And in all three of his verse-dramas he used the *femme fatale*'s cold and ambiguous attractions to express thematic paradoxes: love in death, faith in despair, and illusion in truth.

Lilith begins with a very conventional use of the *femme-fatale* archetype. Lilith is portrayed at first as the incarnation of cold sensuality; her charms are so tainted with evil that a single kiss will bring both rapture and death. But mostly she brings spiritual degradation. In Act I Tancred, the protagonist, both violates his mother's tomb and kills his father for love of the witch, who disappears as soon as he has thus degraded himself. In Act II, seven years later, Tancred dallies with Lilith on an island while his best friend, Gavain, is being murdered on the shore of the lake. And in the third act Tancred marries a Gretchen-like peasant's daughter named Amara, only to grow tired of her within a year. Again Lilith appears to him and tempts him and again Tancred forsakes a loved one. His abandoned wife commits suicide, and Tancred has added yet another blot to his tainted soul. In each of her three appearances to him, Lilith has tormented Tancred by promising and then denying him her body.

Thus during the first three acts Lilith remains the conventional figure of Decadent poetry—the deadly female who embodies a dark, malignant sexuality. Only briefly, in Act I, is her possible philosophical interpretation suggested. She describes herself as dual, a sister to "joy" and "death." And when she persuades Tancred to give her the ruby from his mother's tomb, she attacks his illusions of "reason, duty, love," offering herself instead as an ultimate indulgence of the senses, since, after all, sense experiences are all that men can know of good and evil. But it is primarily in Act IV that Sterling extends his theme beyond the mere drama of temptation that dominates the first three acts. I will discuss this last act in some detail, drawing on both the text and some of Sterling's own comments about his theme.

It is twenty years after the death of his wife, and Tancred has become a sage. He has wandered from Egypt to Cathay, seeking wisdom. For the past seven years he has found refuge in the castle of King Gerbert, where he lives an ascetic's life. Cloistered in a narrow cell, Tancred has devoted years of thought to his effort to find some wisdom which will profit the common man. He is not concerned that the wisdom might prove heretical, although the two servants who are discussing him as the act opens think that he is very unwise. The last course for a simple man, according to the cook, lies in escaping "the doo...s that fall upon the fair and strong. Life is a trap."[2] Sterling wrote to Dreiser regarding this segment that the servants represent the great mass of humanity who care about survival rather than "reform" or "progress."[3] Thus their viewpoint: "Fool: . . . 'I say make others laugh, and they will love you well. So shall you prosper.' Cook: 'Yea, we both delight in men's midriffs. So the cruel arm and eye/Shall spare us. Stroke the lion!'" (p. 75).

Recently. the ageless Lilith has become the mistress of King Gerbert. She renews her assault on the soul of Tancred by making the king suspect that he is a dangerous revolutionary; she persuades Gerbert to have Tancred dine with him, the Archbishop, and the Chancellor the next night—thus they all can examine Tancred for ideas subversive to church or throne. At the dinner (scene 3) Tancred is led to a rash statement that the king's taxations are unfair to his subjects, that their banquet is lavish at the cost of the peasants' hunger. Further, he says that he has "dreamt of years when men shall not be wolves/But brothers." In other words, Tancred has become a Socialist. When Lilith challenges him, he responds:

> Tancred: Is it a dream that there shall come a day
> When one man's joy is not his brothers pain?
> Lilith: It is the very ghost of dreams! Wouldst thou
> dance on Hell's lid, or on its red-hot floor?
> Tancred: I'd do away with Hell. (p. 86)

Lilith answers that Earth *is* Hell; that is what is so charming about it. The fact that a poacher is being flayed alive in the dungeon at that very moment, she says, only makes her admiration of men like Gerbert greater. As for Tancred, if life's injustices bother him, he should trust God. Tancred retorts—

> . . . Leave God to God
> > Let yonder souls smile on the waiting Night—
> > Fed with the lie of immortality;
> > But I smile not. (p. 88)

This is heresy, and the Archbishop is incensed. He asks Tancred to accept the "ancient things" of the church and thereby find peace and joy. Tancred responds,

> > I find them otherwise—
> > Peace but in war against the best of Self,
> > And joy but in the joy one gives mankind.
> > It is thine ancient things that ail— (p. 89)

Though Gerbert is merely amused by Tancred's speech, the Archbishop and Chancellor demand that he be tortured to death. Lilith, of course, agrees, arguing that "this man's word, if loosened on the world,/Will eat like acid all the pomp and power" (p. 90).

Tancred the idealist is ready to die for his beliefs, and he views Death as a welcome oblivion: "For I have walked with masters, men whose words,/Like windows opening on infinity, Show night but not mirage" (p. 92). Before he is dragged to the dungeon, however, Tancred declaims ecstatically about the order of Love that he envisions in the future of human history. In fact, he waxes so rhapsodic in his reformer's zeal that he becomes ridiculous:

> > Ah! human heart!
> So blind! So wise! So base! So beautiful!
> How soon wilt thou be one with all men's hearts?
> What worth to the Adventure—yea, what worth,
> Except it end in Love? And now mine eyes,
> Beholding love beyond these tears of Time,
> Are—

> Gerbert: Is this a feast, or sermon? Drag him out. (p. 95)

In the climactic fourth scene, Tancred is alone in the dungeon, musing on the stars and their message of "man's high homelessness." He is filled with *weltschmertz*, and he agonizes over the nature of men:

> What am I,
> This heart by Time tormented and betrayed,
> And girt by many mysteries? This mote
> Impinged on by infinities? This vast
> Where meet the dark abysses, to become
> A new abyss, that hungers to be filled? (p. 99)

As he thus soliloquizes, Lilith appears to tempt him to renounce his ideals and make his peace with the Archbishop. Tancred refuses to be a traitor to the truth. Scoffing, Lilith grants him a vision of the deepest cosmos, asking him to describe what he sees. Tancred discerns in the vast distance two orbs, one of blood and one of dew:

> And now from each
> Rise vapors, ever denser and more bright.
> They soar, they robe us in magnificence.
> Great chambers open in the splendor, rooms
> Of changing opalescence. Phantom Shapes
> Are dwellers there, that woo and wed and war,
> Mingling in shadow. (p. 104)

Lilith tells him that the orbs are the only real things there; that the "phantom shapes" are illusions. The orbs are pleasure and pain, the source of all human values, of "every thought of good or evil" (p. 104).

Now Lilith reveals to Tancred that not death alone but great pain awaits him. Tomorrow he will be scourged raw and tortured with salt; hours on the rack will end only when he is cooked to death over coals. Tancred resolves nonetheless to cling to his dream of nobler future for man. But Lilith gives him a second vision of the night sky. She proves to him his cosmic insignificance in the eternal recurrence of the universe. Tancred is shaken, but he recoils and resolves to cling to his illusions— to accept his personal pleasures and pains as all the meaning he will find in existence: "I see my rapture and my grief, and

know/That they suffice me. Life, accept this heart/Still hungry
for illusion and for love!" (p. 104). He is weakening.

Lilith seizes the opportunity to tempt Tancred with the illusion of transcendence through rapture. She implores him to
come with her to some never-never land of pleasure, where he
can forget his torment, "couched on the broken rose and lulled
by lutes" (p. 105). Tancred refuses, asserting that Lilith too
is "of illusion," and that he would prefer his illusion of human
dignity to her illusion of joy.

Now Lilith gives him a third vision, an apparition of the end
of the human race, with no "voice/To utter to the vast and voice-
less skies/The words: 'Man was. He suffered. He is not'"
(p. 106). Tancred responds that he will not be discouraged by
this, that the future of mankind still holds a promise that the
"Great Balance" will swing from Pain to Pleasure, that "Free
from the long captivity of self,/The race shall work as one"
(p. 107). This is his final word, and Lilith cannot tempt him
more.

In the last scene of the drama, it is midnight of the next day,
and two of the occupants of the castle, Raoul the troubador
and the servant girl Jehanne, are keeping a love-tryst in a
garden. As they embrace, Jehanne is disturbed by the groans
of Tancred, who is being flayed alive in the dungeon below.
However, she does not protest when Raoul stuffs her ears with
rose-petals and the play ends with their rapturous sighs blended
with Tancred's groans of agony. Thus the ending of the play
provides an ironic commentary on the pleasure-pain discussion
between Tancred and Lilith. Sterling wrote to Dreiser regarding
this final scene, "I ended it with a contrast between pleasure
and pain as indicative of that strangest and most awful of human
faculties, our ability to be happy when we know others are in
agony. I can never forgive myself nor humanity for that."[4]

In the same 1926 letter to Dreiser, Sterling made the best
summary of his sense of the play's theme:

I made the poem moon-haunted, as a symbol of the illusory quality
of love and idealism generally. . . . As to the philosophy of the poem,
which is purely an allegory of temptation, I've let reason and idealism
fight it out, and though so keen a mind as yours can discern that

Lilith has utterly the better of the argument (which is the crux of the poem), yet I have put into the mouth of Tancred the best that can be said for the optimist, and many readers will believe that he is right. I think that is the better way, as denoting the eternal balance between good and evil (pleasure and pain).[5]

In *Lilith*, then, Sterling departed from the conventional treatment of the theme of temptation in Decadent poetry. As the poem moves from the simple seduction scenes in the first acts to the debate between "reason and idealism" in the last, the figure of Lilith gains new symbolic values, and by the end she has become very ambiguous. In the opening scenes she is the familiar *belle dame sans merci*, the "fatal woman" who offers the ecstasy which is death. Later, as "Reason," she contrasts with Tancred's idealism, as she leads him away from his naive faith in humanity and love into an understanding of human insignificance and of the dual principle of pleasure and pain which provides the only source of value in the universe. She is herself Pleasure and Pain, of course, and as she offers Tancred the lie of transcendent raptures, she is illusion. But her final meaning, the meaning which has been implicit throughout the poem, is Despair.

II   *Pleasure and Pain*

After a visit from Dreiser in 1923, Sterling had been prompted to work on an essay which would outline in prose the thoughts behind *Lilith* and many of his other recent poems. This essay, entitled "Life," "Implications of Infinity," and finally "Pleasure and Pain," he never published.[6] Nevertheless, as an attempt to reconcile the nebular hypothesis with his neo-Epicurean principle of pleasure and pain, it is more representative of Sterling's philosophical position in his later years than any other work.

The essay begins with a simple statement of the supremacy of scientific truth: man has invented gods time and again, only to find that science negates his gods. Astronomy especially "has at last become the sunlight to melt the black fog of superstition in which humanity is still enveloped." Sterling describes the immensity of the known universe, the enormous distances and

numbers of stars, and points out that even science is limited in
its ability to identify what must be only a part of the infinity
of space. Here the thoughtful mind must move beyond the realm
of the observable and meditate on the implications of infinity;
Sterling moves to a statement of the nebular hypothesis, the
theory of the eternal death and rebirth of stars, presented as a
logical condition of a universe which is infinite in both space
and time.

Sterling then attacks those who believe in a beginning and
an end to the universe: "Certain thoughtless minds have, indeed,
in the past, conceived of an infinite and omnipotent power that
formed, at some remote date, the material universe, and who,
after an indefinite period, will cause that 'the heavens be rolled
up as a scroll.' One does not deny these high-priests of the
teleology their conception of an acrobatic and drama-producing
god, nor their ability to imagine that an infinite mind could be
capable of a whimsy, for that is all that any such action, limited
by time, however vast, would be."

Returning to the recurrence of stars, Sterling attacks another
manifestation of man's pride—his conviction that life is unique
and that it is moving toward a great destiny. This is not so:
human life is caught in the same process of disintegration and
rebirth as everything else, and of course is much more limited
in scope than suns, because of the very limited range of light,
heat, and moisture in which life can exist. Thus far Sterling
has merely stated in prose the argument of **"The Testimony of
the Suns."** But here he shifts his argument, moving from the
"implications of infinity" statement to another part of his thesis:
pleasure and pain. He rejects the Schopenhauerean will-to-live
argument for life's origin and substitutes a simple Epicurean
principle: 'Can one rationally believe that the first forms of Life
absorbed nutriment with the knowledge that so doing would
enable them to live? It is more reasonable to suppose that there
were any will at all exerted, it was put forth for the satisfaction
afforded by such absorption of nutriment—i.e., for pleasure."
He goes on to reject the idea of the human personality—it is an
ephemeron, masking only subjective sensations of pleasure and
pain, which "being non-illusory, partake of the nature of the

Absolute, of that which has been for all eternity, is self sustaining, and will be forever."

Continuing this line of thought, Sterling asserts that truth (other than mathematical), beauty, good and evil, and all such terms which denote abstract values are only synonyms for pleasure and pain. "It is from our sensations, painful or otherwise, that we have derived what we are pleased to call our souls. . . . The universe *is*. It is the Absolute. It needs have no meaning in itself. And its importance to man exists in such degree as it renders him pleasure or pain." The pleasure-pain principle is directly applicable to the human will. Schopenhauer is wrong: human beings "exist not to escape pain but to embrace pleasure." If life were "merely an effort to flee from pain," many would simply take their lives.

Sterling ridicules the reformers who, in attempting to achieve Utopian goals, "might as well . . . endeavor to free the race from pain." But, like a true relativist, he remarks that we should not abandon efforts to achieve the ideal "if we find joy in those efforts." And it will detract from our pain if we realize that the effort is what is worthwhile to us, the goal an illusion.

At present, pain overshadows pleasure in the world. The order of Nature is based upon pain, and man is more atrocious than the brutes: "he confronts the tragedies of human existence with a creditable uneasiness, and endeavors to excuse them in various quaint theogonies. However, his dismay at such disconcertive phenomena does not deter him from being the only brute that enslaves his own kind!"

The essay ends with a diatribe against the competitive system and its injustices—the tendency to award pleasure to the few, pain to the many. Sterling concludes with a hope that man will be able to overcome his selfishness and attempt to "light as far as possible the shadowed and bloodstained paths of life."

"Pleasure and Pain," then, is an attempt to tie together into a single statement three divergent strands of Sterling's thought: the astronomical speculations which had prompted "The Testimony of the Suns," the pleasure-pain principle which he had come to believe supersedes all other ethical categories, and the desire for a change in the social system to create more nearly equal possibilities for the happiness of all men.

The contradictions inherent in this attempt to tie together divergent ideas were not really resolved. If the pleasure principle is as basic as Sterling contends, for instance, then the vision of an ideal state should be as ridiculous as Christianity. But Sterling did not believe the last part of his own essay. He wrote to several friends that he had made a much stronger statement in behalf of reformers than he personally believed, and that the end of the essay was not really representative of his views. His nihilism was too severe to be communicated to more innocent minds, he contended: "I've conjured up such a cosmic nightmare that I thought it needed a little amelioration. I don't care to afflict my fellows with the full weight of my pessimism."[7]

Sterling's cynicism was indeed much deeper than ever before. In 1925, when he wrote a memoir of Bierce for the *American Mercury*, he remarked that "Bierce's pessimism was, like Twain's, of the sophomoric order, concerned with the immediate state of mankind, and innocent of the implications of infinity, not to mention those of relativity."[8] And in the last two years of his life, Sterling assaulted American civilization from his "Rhymes and Reactions" column of the *Overland Monthly*, in terms which express an extreme misanthropy:

A strong race, a strong and terrible race! Notorious for one justice for the rich, another for the poor, saturated with a million weird superstitions, bigoted from dandruff to toenails, intolerant to the point of deadly menace, lawless until old age, bilious with hatred of new ideas and the mental function generally, idiotic with worship of mere physical prowess, idolizers of the mahouds of the movies, scornful of all it cannot comprehend, pleasure-mad and crazed for comfort, sex-besotted to an unimaginable and unprintable degree, maggoty with graft, driven like so many sheep by the vast and complacent powers that hold them in unrealized bondage, vacuum-worshippers and adorers of every jitney messiah that appears—and crucifiers of those that have any claim to respect, haters of beauty, even subconsciously, swift to enthrone the false god and as swift to cut him down, with all possible cruelty, blinded, fearful, mentally deliquescent, hypocritical above all other tribes of history—I refer, of course, to that deplorable people, the head-hunters and cannibals of the Solomon Islands. We cannot too sadly lament the conditions in which it has pleased the Divine Power to place them, even as we look forward to the happy time when we shall have brought them the blessings of American civilization.[9]

And yet in many of these late works Sterling seems to be deliberately restraining himself, holding back from the full expression of his despair. As he wrote in a posthumously published poem, "The Wiser Prophet":

> I will be wise, and show the people not
> The shadows of the menace I foresee.
> Nay, let them dance, and let the sun-duped throng
> Make merry with its harlots to the last.[10]

In the above and in many other passages of Sterling's late writings there are premonitions of his end, and it is tempting to see in the statement in "Pleasure and Pain"—"escape from the ultimate horrors of pain is, or should be, a wiser action than pursuit of the unsatisfying and transitory phantoms of pleasure" —a philosophical justification for his suicide.

III Rosamund

The historical drama *Rosamund* (1920) is a departure from the imaginary settings and heavily allegorical symbols that Sterling employed in *Lilith*. Sterling was fascinated by the account of Rosamund in Gibbon's *Decline and Fall of the Roman Empire;* the dramatic possibilities of the four murders and the rape suggested a sensational tragedy of revenge in the Elizabethan manner, and the figure of Rosamund herself fascinated him as another version of the Lilith-figure. In this poem, however, Sterling chose to treat her as a kind of savage innocent, a woman trapped by her own beauty in a barbaric world. Accordingly, Sterling structured the first two acts around a series of intolerable choices that Rosamund is forced to make, and in the final act he dramatized how she herself becomes infected by the brutality she abhors.

The drama opens at the court of Turisund, King of the Gepidae. Alboin, the son of Andoin, King of the Lombards, has defeated Turisund in battle and has come to demand tribute. Alboin has killed Harra, Turisund's son, and the other son, Cumimund, refuses to feast with him. When Alboin arrogantly demands his spoil of victory, the dead Harra's cuirass, Turisund, weeping, accedes. A little later, Alboin meets Rosamund, the eighteen-year-old daughter of Cumimund. He is entranced by her beauty and despite her obvious disgust he demands of Cumimund her hand in marriage. Cumimund refuses.

But a year later Alboin, now king of the Lombards, captures Rosamund in a raid. In spite of her helplessness she defies him, and he rapes her brutally. A month later, Alboin is captured by Cumimund, who plans to castrate him for his rape of Rosamund. But Alboin persuades Cumimund to let Rosamund decide whether he should be unmanned or be set free under tribute and dishonor. Torn with indecision, Rosamund finally decides to set him free; she cannot be responsible for Alboin's suffering.

Her charity, however, goes unrewarded. Once again Alboin goes to war against the Gepidae, and this time he vanquishes them completely. Cumimund is dead and Rosamund once again is a captive. When she refuses to marry him, Alboin offers her another intolerable choice: either marry or be given to three horrible hunchbacks. Only because she is pregnant, Rosamund is forced to choose Alboin; she prays for a son to avenge her.

In the second act Alboin continues his degradation of Rosamund. Drinking at the table with his knights, he forces her to quaff wine from a skull-cup, then tells her that it is her father's skull. Again she must choose: either drink or be taken away from her infant daughter; she drinks.

Until this point Rosamund has been portrayed entirely as the unwilling victim of the cruel Alboin. In the middle of the second act, however, she begins to assume the role of avenger. Lacking a son who can become her hope for vengeance, Rosamund acquires a lover, Alboin's armor-bearer, Helmichis. She persuades Helmichis to assassinate Alboin and seduces Peredeus, the lover of her maid, in order to gain his help. Then, when Rosamund and Alboin are alone in his chamber, she binds his sword into its sheath. Sleepy from drink, Alboin does not notice it until Helmichis and Peredeus enter to kill him. Rosamund mockingly drinks wine from the skull-cup while Alboin dies from a sword-wound in the loins.

In the last act the focus is more directly on Rosamund as a woman trapped in a brutal world, and forced to utilize that brutality to gain her ends. She has fled with Alboin's treasure to Ravenna, and appeals for safety to Longinus, the exarch and minister of Emperor Justin. Longinus is immediately infatuated with Rosamund, but, unlike Alboin, he promises to treat her gently. She accepts him, but realizes that now she must find a way out of her entanglements with Peredeus and Helmichis. She maneuvers Longinus into having Peredeus murdered, and when Helmichis refuses to leave her in spite of her offer of half of Alboin's treasure, she poisons him. Before he dies, Helmichis forces her to drink the poison also, and the drama ends.

In several soliloquies in the last act, Rosamund expresses her longing for a world of peace, not for herself but for her daughter. She is clearly a victim of her own barbaric times, forced to use whatever tools come to hand in her attempt to provide a brighter future for her daughter. But she becomes infected by the cruelty of the methods she must use. By extension, the drama is a parable of the destruction of innocence, and the way all attempts to gain happiness only lead to greater pain. Further, Rosamund reflects Sterling's cynicism regarding the ability of mankind to recognize beauty and to revere it for itself, instead of degrading it through attempts to dominate and possess it. This last theme is also a major element of the allegorical *Truth*, published in 1923.

IV Truth

The verse-drama *Truth*, the last major work published in Sterling's lifetime, appeared in book form in 1923, and a revised version was performed successfully by the Bohemian Club in 1926. Though the play was not produced again, and the published dramatic poem attracted little critical attention, it is one of Sterling's finest works. In the frontispiece to the printed edition of the Bohemian Club version Sterling wrote that the drama is "an allegory of [Truth's] fate at the hands of a populace, showing how she is first crucified, then worshiped, then rejected."[11] The overall scheme of *Truth* conforms to this conception; however, the ambiguity of the Truth figure and the varying responses of those most sympathetic to her make the theme more subtle and complex.

As the drama begins, Perroh, a guard at the ramparts of the city Vae, and Egon, a poet and cynic, witness a strange couple approaching the city at dawn. When the gates are opened and the two are admitted, there is a public furor. Uliun the Dreamer, a local madman, has brought an unknown nude girl of transcendent loveliness to the city. The girl seems mute, but she has terrible eyes. Uliun claims that she spoke to him in the mountains where he found her, "in an alien tongue/Of chiming silver and of dripping gems" (p. 17). Uliun will not allow her to be covered; he wants the people to worship her as he does, but the mob, excited by her nakedness, clamors that she is a harlot. Eor, the captain of the guard, cloaks her and conducts the two to Uliun's home. But Uliun's wife turns them both away, and it is decided that they should be lodged in the jail until king Ducorial can see them.

At the jail, the three guards throw lots for the first chance to molest the strange girl. But each who enters the cell returns ashen-white from fear of her terrible eyes. Egon himself arrives, enters her cell, and returns white-faced like the others. Shortly after, he goes alone into the mountains.

The next day, Uliun and the girl are brought before the judge Hothrundus. Uliun protests that she is "of the gods," but Hothrundus concludes that she is a witch. The two are sentenced to be lashed and driven from the city, but a messenger from the tyrant Ducorial halts the punishment. Summoned before Ducorial, Uliun tells how he first encountered the mysterious girl in the mountains. A mood of transcendence, bred of "the night's infinity," had fallen upon him. When he came to himself, the girl was near him, whispering untranslatable secrets of "God's silence, and the world's enormous pain,/ Forevermore unbroken" (p. 50). Since then, Uliun concludes, he has become her disciple. Ducorial, however, is only interested in her physical beauty; he sends Uliun to prison and has the girl taken to his own chambers.

In the next scene, Arkonion, the high-priest, is standing before the huge statue of the god Korkamedum. He soliloquizes about the impermanence of religions and civilizations:

Thy temple-gloom

Gives the same answer unto the same prayer—
A silence. Is it well the gods should speak?
But if a man, as I, speak in thy name,
Shall not the people prosper, and thy house?
By thee our fathers rose; by thee their sons
Abide a little, ere new nations carve
New cities from the old basalt. But Life,
Victim of an unalterable rite,
Forever bleeds. Tho priest and god are dead
At long-forsaken altars: she endures.
Fair is the mask a moment, and the lie. (p. 55)

Suddenly the priest Horeth enters, announcing the death of
Ducorial, mysteriously stricken in his chambers at the feet of
the strange maiden. Arkonion resolves to torture the truth from
her, as the scene ends.

By this point in the play the allegory has become obvious.
The young girl, of course, is Truth. The persistent attempts by
the townspeople, the soldiers, and the king to defile the Truth
only lead to their own bafflement and annihilation. Uliun is
one of those visionaries who think they know a portion of Truth
and devote themselves to communicating it to an ignorant and
profane world, yet the words of truth to Uliun—"God's silence
and the world's enormous pain"—reflect the same despair that
lies at the center of *Lilith* and "Pleasure and Pain." In the second
major action of the drama, Sterling shows how Truth is in turn
martyred and deified by a multitude who are ignorant of its
real nature; and, with a turn of irony, he reveals how true
knowledge can only lead to death.

With Ducorial's demise, high priest Arkonion rules the king-
dom. He decides to have Uliun put to death, and he resolves
that the girl, with her strange powers, must become the "hand
maiden" to the god Korkamedum. But first Arkonion sends
her to the fire torture to confess the manner of the king's death.
The fire does not burn her, however, and the priest who took
her to the torture room goes mad. The next day Uliun is crucified before a populace who will not listen to him when he tries

to tell them of Truth. To Arkonion, however, Uliun is able to
talk of his devotion:

> For Beauty is of good, howe'er she hide
> Her face with Evil's mask a while. My death
> Is near, but I have served her in my life,
> And tho men say I have not served her well,
> I shall not know, or knowing shall not care,
> Who am but shadow of her starriness.
> *Arkonion*: And to what end?
> *Uliun*:   There is no end. Her light
> Shall be on other heavens. To have seen,
> Suffices.
> *Arkonion*: She is Beauty, then?
> *Uliun*:   The heart
> Of Beauty, which is Truth.
> *Arkonion*:   What is her word?
> *Uliun*: Her word is of man's pain. I will not say
> The whole, lest thou pervert it. She will speak
> Through greater lips than mine. (pp. 69–70)

Uliun's words point out an important characteristic of Sterling's enigmatic Truth. As an allegorical figure, she is the
embodiment of an apparent contradiction. If Truth is "the
heart of Beauty" and her word is "of man's pain," then human
misery and Beauty must be compatible. For Uliun, apparently,
this is so. Thus he is not the Platonist that he would seem to be.
He is able to tolerate a contradiction that broke Tancred in
Lilith; and if there is a way of reconciling the contradiction,
it must lie in a realm beyond all human values. Truth's other-
worldly beauty, her terrifying eyes, and her supernatural powers,
all imply the existence of such a realm, and Uliun is alluding
to it when he speaks of his attraction toward death:

> Ever strange voices call me, and I go
> On roads of dream austere and desolate. (p. 69)

As Truth is thrown from a cliff at Arkonion's orders, Uliun dies
on his cross. The stewardship of Truth has only brought death

for him, as the abuse of Truth brought madness and death for the others.

Uliun's mistake becomes more apparent as Egon the cynic watches the sacrifice from his mountainside. He has seen the eyes of Truth and, like Uliun, thinks her a goddess. He is horrified at the depravity he witnesses, but neither her beauty nor his disgust at the sacrilege of casting her from the cliffs blinds him to Truth's essentially inhuman and evil nature: "The Dream is evil, and the Dream endures!" (p. 83).

Egon's suspicion notwithstanding, the reappearance of Truth at the city gates, unharmed and mute as ever, creates a different sort of uproar among the populace. Believing now that she is a goddess, the people bear her to the temple, where they clamor for the overthrow of the priests. Arkonion exhorts his priests to help him outwit the mob:

> Is it for this that ye have pondered much,
> And read our ancient scrolls, and learned the fate
> Of Truth among the nations? She is stoned,
> Except she came to them in pleasing garb,
> With honey in her mouth, and 'round her head
> Hope's iris. If she seek them otherwise,
> As now, with eyes that trouble and arraign,
> And flesh that hath no share in mystery,
> She shall be slain, or stoned, or cast aside
> As one of little worth. (pp. 110–11)

Arkonian has the statue of Korkamedum toppled from its altar; then he stabs the girl to the heart and has her taken away to be trussed and set in the god's place. In the revised 1926 edition, Arkonion now apostrophizes to Truth with full understanding of her ambiguity:

> O changeless Truth, child of eternity,
> Whose ghost is worshiped and denied by Time!
> Marble and mist of dreams we dare not dream!
> Medusa of the light, whose deadly gaze
> Shall turn the spirit, not the flesh, to stone!
> Abiding shadow of the infinite!
> Terror immortal, twin-born with the sun

From night's abyss! Why do men seek thy face?
For they that find thee shall not know they find;
For they that find thee shall be changed. Their hearts
Shall ache with loneliness to see thy face
Among the stars, more beautiful than they—
Among the stars, but colder than all stars,
A phantom and a goddess and a fire. [12]

Like Uliun, Arkonion realizes the combination of despair and longing that Truth inspires, but like Egon he understands her destructive, life-denying power. Yet he also knows that the essence of priestcraft is to create illusions for the multitude to worship in the name of truth.

Satirical references to the Christian Church help to reinforce the point, as Arkonion's priests drape the mummified corpse of Truth with seven sacred veils. Arkonion dictates the careful placement of the body between the altars:

These our silks
Shall lure his gaze who else would scan her face
Too shrewdly. As she gleams before you now,
So shall the world behold her, nor detect
The mummy swathed in spendors. If she stink,
Burn incense, that its wafture on the gloom
May work a fragrant sorcery, and rouse
The eternal acquiescence of the sense. (p. 114)

Arkonion's stratagem is a success; as the people burst into the palace to kill the priests of Korkamedum, they find their new goddess enshrined before them.

In the last scene of the drama, Egon is on his hillside with the beautiful shepherdess Dendra. They watch as the broken statue of Korkamedum is pushed over the cliff from which Truth had fallen the day before, and they see the advancing hostile host of Corvannon, an army far too great to be resisted by Vae. Egon and Dendra are in love, and though love is fleeting, Egon finds it best: "I turn to thee and find/The grief and rapture of the Here and Now,/Knowing that Here and Now for us are all"; (pp. 122–23). But suddenly on the hillside above him Egon sees the shining figure of Truth, beckoning him to the mountains. He refuses to follow, as he had fled from her gaze before. After she vanishes beyond the crest of the hill, Egon explains to Dendra,

> She is not
> For me. In thine illusion, not in hers,
> I seek nepenthe, drowning at thy breast.
> Her home is but the wind upon the snows,
> Or the cold star above them. 'Tis on thine
> That I would know forgetfulness or death. (p. 124)

Like Tancred in *Lilith*, Egon has chosen to embrace a chimera. When Lilith showed him despair, Tancred chose to cling to the illusion of human dignity. Here Egon chooses the illusion of love over the illusion of transcendent Truth, as the poem ends.

In fact, all the responses to Truth dramatized in the poem are different types of illusions. In the beginning, the townspeople, the soldiers, the judge, and the king only see a beautiful naked form. Ignorant and brutal, they try to dominate without understanding, and are soon confounded. Uliun the Dreamer, on the other hand, understands a little of her language, but insists on distorting her message of pain and despair into a sort of mystical optimism. Thus he worships a lie. Arkonion the high priest, a man of perception and a complete cynic, recognizes the terrible capability of Truth to "turn spirit to stone." He sees her power to overthrow him, and thus he consciously creates a lie which men can worship and call truth. And finally, as a poet Egon should follow Truth, and he is summoned by her at the end of the poem. But he chooses the lie of love, because Truth's ministry is no service at all—it is despair and death.

The Figure of Truth, as Sterling develops her, is perfectly suited to his theme of illusion. She is beautiful but pale—like a corpse. Her strange muteness and even stranger passivity allow people to understand her according to their own nature, and her most active feature—the terrible eyes—brings not understanding but fear, madness, and death. Truth's essence, it is implied, is beyond our comprehension but horrible, and all her attributes combine to make her the symbol of a numbing void at the center of life. Thus the degree to which she is seen as divine, exalted, or ennobling is the poem's final illusion.

CHAPTER 7

Conclusion

WITHIN fifteen years following his death, Sterling's poetry fell into the near obscurity in which it has remained until the present. The difficulty of obtaining most of his poems—privately published in limited editions—is partly responsible, but more so are the negative assessments of his work by Louis Untermeyer and Harriet Monroe (cited earlier). Yet the truest reason for Sterling's obscurity lies in the swift changes which took place in American poetry during his lifetime. A Decadent poet in the age of Imagism—who would seem more obsolete?

Accordingly, the literary historians who have assessed Sterling's career have relegated him to the "twilight interval," the transitional phase of American poetry which preceded the Imagist rebellion. Alfred Kreymborg, for example, rates Sterling's gifts as highly as those of Edgar Lee Masters or William Vaughn Moody, but discusses his poetry as "a tragic epitome of the adventure of many American poets among books and bookishness."[1] Horace Gregory and Maurya Zaturenska group him with Joaquin Miller and Edwin Markham as West Coast poets, and although they consider Sterling the most talented of the three, they stress his faults of rhetoric and archaistic diction. Yet they make a potentially penetrating comment: "Underlying Sterling's reaches toward floating planets and wild constellations, there was a persistent note of pathos as well as a fitfully expressed sense of evil. Unlike Markham and unlike Miller, he seemed to feed the presence of a darkness, a Spenglerian melodrama that Jeffers was to enter and explore."[2]

More recently, Stanton Coblentz's "George Sterling: Western Phenomenon" praises the same qualities which the new poets of the 1920s had condemned: "His is the grand manner and at times the grandiloquent style; his is the cosmic perspective,

156

which is not content merely with noting the convolutions of the *I* in man, but looks upon our species against the background of the worlds and ages, with a judgment that at times may seem impassive and pitiless, but that can be vibrant and resplendent."[3] Coblentz, it must be noted, is a remarkably conservative critic who reserves his highest admiration for the poetic achievements of the Victorians.

Most contemporary literary historians, however, either completely ignore Sterling or grant him the briefest of citations. A typical treatment in the recent *History of Modern Poetry* by David Perkins (Cambridge, 1976), which discusses his poetry in a single short paragraph. And social historian Henry May, in his excellent *The End of American Innocence* (New York, 1959), only mentions Sterling once in passing, despite the obvious ways in which Sterling's career is a vindication of May's thesis that the process of American cultural alienation, the "decline or partial disintegration of belief,"[4] was not, as formerly supposed, a phenomenon of the postwar 1920's but was well under way before 1917.

It is as a Bohemian rather than as a poet that Sterling has received the most attention. Miriam Allen deFord, in *They Were San Franciscans*, Emily Hahn, in *Romantic Rebels*, and Albert Parry, in *Garrets and Pretenders* all present Sterling as a symbol of the pre-earthquake San Francisco Bohemia, and Parry assigns him a central role in the history of American Bohemianism—a position which is well affirmed by the events of his life. And thus, if Sterling is discussed at all, it is either as a Bohemian or in connection with more famous writers like Bierce, London, or Dreiser, whose biographers often provide good insights into his personality but understandably have little to say about his poems. What then, is Sterling's true position in the history of American poetry?

We might find a partial answer by turning to an early essay, "George Sterling's Place in Modern Poetry," by Lionel Stevenson (*University of California Chronicle*, 1929). Stevenson begins his discussion by pointing out that Sterling's poetry is not at all "essentially American." The only appropriate approach to an understanding of his achievement would be through comparing his work to the English poetry which inspired him. In Steven-

son's opinion, Sterling assimilated three major features of nineteenth-century poetry: Romantic escapism, Victorian preoccupation with science and religion, and Pre-Raphaelite or Decadent
aestheticism. Sterling did not, however, absorb Browning's vein
of psychological realism, nor did he allow his verse to approach
too closely to personal statement. As Stevenson puts it, "his
inmost self being never allowed explicit utterance, the reader
has the interest of seeking to discern it beneath the convolutions
of the robe. Such indirection may prevent Sterling from achieving the transcendant power of the greatest poetry, but it offers
the double pleasure of its external richness of beauty and its
tantalizing hints of the strange and tragic identity within."[5]
   Summarizing the characteristics of Sterling's poems—the tech-
nical skill and wealth of imagery, the quest for fleeting beauty,
the conscious relinquishment of "poetry of the human touch,"
and the conflict between aestheticism and Socialist political sympathies—Stevenson concludes that Sterling's most persistent tone
is pessimistic, and that his ultimate "creed . . . is one of resig-
nation and fatalism. Neither affirming nor denying, he counsels
passivity as the sole means of enduring life, with escape into
the frankly unreal realm of fantasy as the only anodyne."[6]
Finally, Stevenson declares that Sterling "saved an era of his
nation's literature from entire provincialism," and asserts that
the reason Sterling failed to be recognized adequately was his
alienation on one hand from the *avant-garde*—because of his
technique—and on the other from the conventional, bourgeois
reader—because of his pessimism.
   Stevenson's essay is by far the most perceptive assessment of
Sterling's poetic achievement that has yet appeared. It is the
only attempt to examine the entire range of his poetry, and it
is the only criticism which recognizes the uniqueness of Sterling's position in *fin-de-siècle* American poetry. Like most of the
criticism which is friendly to Sterling, it tends to gloss over
some of his faults—the bombast of his more grandiose style,
for example. It has a strong bias against the new poetry and
tends to regard Sterling as a lingering holdout against a generally undesirable trend—a view with which Sterling undoubtedly
would have agreed, but which now seems rather reactionary.
Because the essay concentrates on earlier poems, it does not

adequately stress the depth of Sterling's pessimism, and, like all other critics of Sterling, Stevenson makes the assumption that he exercised no literary influence on the new poets.

The last assumption would seem to be true: serious poets of the 1920s and 1930s avoided any use of the rhetorical effects which dominated Sterling's verse, and Decadent poetry evolved into ornate prose fantasy in the manner of Clark Ashton Smith (Sterling's protégé) or H. P. Lovecraft. Yet one modern poet of note might have been influenced by Sterling, and that is Robinson Jeffers.

The personal relationship between Sterling and Jeffers has already been mentioned. Sterling was one of the first to "discover" Jeffers's poetry, and with his *Robinson Jeffers: The Man and the Artist* (1926) he helped establish him as a major new poet. Until his death in 1926, Sterling was one of Jeffers's few personal friends. Yet the depth of their friendship is uncertain and problematic. Jeffer's biographer Melba Barrett Bennett, for example, comments that Jeffers "only accepted Sterling as he would the scenery. He [Jeffers] was strangely incapable of responding to friendship. He felt admiration and even affection for a few persons, but any effort to keep the relationship warm depended entirely on Una [Jeffers's wife] or the friend."[7]

But others who have written about Sterling and Jeffers have suggested that a deeper relationship may have existed between them. Ann Ridgeway, editor of Jeffers's letters, writes of the "reach of their brief and curiously detached friendship in which each respected the other's work, personality and opinions but was very little influenced by any of them." She goes on to say that "the friendship did lead J[effers] into further self-evaluation—prepared him for many explanations his work began to demand."[8] This last is quite clear from the many letters Jeffers wrote to Sterling which attempt to justify his use of certain motifs in his poems. And finally, the author of a recent book on Jeffers, Alex Vardamis, comments that "the relationship between Jeffers and Sterling deserves additional biographical investigation. It is here sufficient to note that the suicide of Mr. Sterling . . . greatly saddened Jeffers and perhaps led him even further into misanthropy and isolation."[9] To explore the last comment would be beyond the scope of this work, but we might speculate that Jeffers's friendship with Sterling is an indication not only of Jeffers's gratitude and Sterling's generosity, but of an influence which may be Sterling's primary legacy to modern poetry

Despite the obvious differences in poetics, a reader of Jeffers's poems might be struck by a certain affinity with Sterling's more austere poems about vultures, stars, or the ocean. Jeffers's sense of "the impersonal power of nature" is similar to Sterling's treatment of the cold and inhuman truths of the universe. And when Jeffers writes of stars, for example, there is always a sentiment similar to Sterling's:

> The universe expands and contracts like a great heart.
> It is expanding, the farthest nebulae
> Rush with the speed of light into empty space.
> It will contract, the immense navies of stars and
>   galaxies, dust-clouds and nebulae
> Are recalled home . . .
>   . . . new universes
> Jewel the black breast of night; and far off the
>   outer nebulae like charging spearmen again
> Invade emptiness.[10]

Repeatedly in his poems Jeffers uses astronomical imagery to underscore his sense of the total inconsequentiality of man—precisely as Sterling did, but with a power of language which Sterling could not achieve.

In the best work of both poets there is a lofty pessimism and a reverence for a cold, inhuman principle of beauty. But Jeffers uses concrete objects—hawks and stone—to symbolize the terrible power of the inanimate earth, with an intensity which Sterling's conceits, borrowed from the stockpile of the Decadent poets, could not convey.

Nevertheless, there is evidence that Jeffers had admired the work of Sterling for many years, perhaps even to the point of veneration. In his first letter to Sterling, he remarked, "You have long been a fixed star in my sky—since for my delight I came upon Wine of Wizardry in some magazine many years ago—and living about Carmel the past ten years I have felt myself again and again an intruder in your domain, but now the lord of the region has made me welcome."[11] It is quite possible that Jeffers, living in Carmel for many years as he developed his poetic voice, might have felt Sterling's influence almost environmentally. Sterling was the recognized laureate of the region, and Jeffers was the neophyte. And even though Jeffers was compelled to reject the Decadent tradition, which in his view had become "slight and fantastic, abstract, unreal, eccentric,"[12] he still may have felt an affinity with Sterling, who before him had one of the most antisentimental voices in American poetry.

And it is in that rejection of the sentimental, in that strain of pessimism which Jeffers admired, that we may establish Sterling's most significant literary achievement. Aside from the possibility that he may arguably have influenced Robinson Jeffers, Sterling made a tangible contribution of his own. The contradictions he faced in attempting to reconcile Decadence with Naturalism and socialism with aestheticism tell us a great deal about the artistic dilemmas of his times. Stevenson is right in asserting that Sterling was noteworthy in his effort to perpetuate the English Romantic tradition, but more importantly, he was one of the first American poets to base an artistic vision on the failure of human progress and the need to confront radical despair. Though Sterling may remain best known for his remarkable personal relationships with other writers and for his role in the history of American Bohemianism, he should also be known as an important transitional poet, who, attempting to reconcile nineteenth-century poetic theory with a distinctly twentieth-century sense of alienation, helped prepare the way for the emergence of Modernism in America.

Notes and References

Chapter One

1. "A Memoir of Ambrose Bierce," in *The Letters of Ambrose Bierce*, ed. Bertha Clark Pope (New York, 1967), p. xxxvii.
2. "A First-Class Fighting Man," *American Mercury* 10 (January 1927): 76.
3. Details of Dr. Sterling's life are drawn from his obituary in the *New York Times*, March 10, 1897, p. 7.
4. "Fighting Man," p. 76.
5. Robert O'Brien, "Riptides," *San Francisco Chronicle*, December 7, 1949, p. 22.
6. Ibid.
7. O'Brien, "Riptides," December 1, 1949, p. 18.
8. John C. Huden, "George Sterling, Prankster-Poet," *Long Island Forum*, December 1943, p. 163.
9. This comment is made by, among others, Carey McWilliams, "George Sterling," *Dictionary of American Biography*, 17, p. 586; and Michael Orth, "A Biography of George Sterling," M.A. thesis, San Francisco State College, 1963, p. 6.
10. G. H. Cunningham, " 'Reg'lar Feller,' " *Saturday Review of Literature* 6 (July 27, 1929): 12.
11. Clarence H. Wilson, "Sterling and P.J.," *Saturday Review of Literature* 6 (August 10, 1929): 44.
12. William McDevitt, *My Father, Father Tabb* (San Francisco, 1945), p. 85.
13. Ibid.
14. Ibid.
15. The following details of Tabb's life are drawn from *Dictionary of American Biography*, IX, p. 262.
16. Edward O'Day, "1869–1926," *Overland Monthly* 85, no. 12 (December 1927): 327.
17. George Sterling, *The Testimony of the Suns and Other Poems* (San Francisco, 1903), p. 121.
18. Sterling, "Fighting Man," p. 80.
19. O'Brien, "Riptides," December 5, 1949, p. 21.

20. Orth, p. 23, quoting a radio script prepared by Samuel Dickinson, October 25, 1946, Albert Bender Room, Stanford University Library.

21. Joan D. Berbrick, ed., *Sounds and Sweet Airs: The Poetry of Long Island* (Port Washington, N.Y., 1970), p. 127.

22. *Who Was Who in America*, I (Chicago, 1942), p. 535.

23. Carey McWilliams, "Roosevelt Johnson Becomes Reminiscent," *Overland Monthly* 85, no. 12 (December 1927): 367.

24. George Sterling, "Joaquin Miller," *American Mercury* 7 (February 1926): 223.

25. "The Shadow Maker," *American Mercury* 6 (September 1925): 12.

26. Ibid., p. 10.

27. A discussion of the early literary history of San Francisco can be found in Franklin Walker, *San Francisco's Literary Frontier* (New York, 1939), passim.

28. For a discussion of the Montgomery Block Bohemia, see Idwal Jones, *Ark of Empire* (Garden City, N.Y., 1951), passim.

29. Dalton Harvey Gross, ed., "The Letters of George Sterling," doctoral dissertation, Southern Illinois University, 1968, p. 12.

30. Joan London, *Jack London and His Times* (New York, 1939), p. 259.

31. "Of America," *A Wine of Wizardry and Other Poems* (San Francisco, 1909), pp. 60–61.

32. Will Irwin, *The Making of a Reporter* (New York, 1942), p. 89.

33. Ibid., p 90.

34. Richard O'Connor, *Jack London* (Boston, 1964), pp. 113–31 passim.

35. Ibid., p 259.

36. Jack London, *Martin Eden* (New York, 1908), p, 277.

37. Ibid., p. 279.

38. Ibid., p. 289.

39. Ibid., p. 374.

40. O'Connor, p. 160.

41. Joan London makes this speculation; *Jack London and His Times*, p. 260.

42. For a description of Coppa's, see Warren Unna, *The Coppan Murals* (San Francisco, 1952), passim.

43. Ibid., p. 17.

44. Sterling to Margaret Cobb Smith, August 9, 1924; Stanford University Library.

45. Mary Austin, "George Sterling at Carmel," *American Mercury* 11 (May 1927): 69.

46. Joseph Noel, *Footloose in Arcadia: A Personal Record of Jack London, George Sterling, and Ambrose Bierce* (New York, 1940), p. 53.

47. "Sanctuary," *Selected Poems* (New York, 1923), p. 30.

Chapter Two

1. For a detailed account of the creation of the Carmel colony, see Franklin Dickinson Walker, *The Seacoast of Bohemia* (San Francisco, 1966), passim.

2. Sterling to Bierce (n.d.), quoted by Walker, p. 14.

3. Ibid., p. 15.

4. Mary Austin, *Earth Horizons* (New York, 1932), pp. 298–99.

5. The five Sterling Carmel diaries contain an account of the daily weather and a record of visitors to the colony; they are deposited in the Bancroft Library, University of California at Berkeley.

6. Sterling to London, July 31, 1906, "Letters of George Sterling," p. 77.

7. Arnold Genthe, *As I Remember* (New York, 1941), pp. 75–76.

8. "The Abalone Song," broadside published by Albert Bender, 1937.

9. Mary Austin, "A Poet in Outland," *Overland Monthly* 35 (November 1927): 351.

10. "George Sterling at Carmel," *American Mercury* 11 (May 1927): 72.

11. *Cosmopolitan* 43 (September 1907): 551.

12. Ibid., p. 576.

13. *Cosmopolitan* 44 (December 1907): 223.

14. Sterling to London, September 12, 1907, "Letters of George Sterling," p. 98.

15. *A Wine of Wizardry and Other Poems* (San Francisco, 1909), p. 87.

16. Richard O'Connor, *Jack London*, p. 376.

17. *The Autobiography of Upton Sinclair* (London, 1962), p. 161.

18. Mark Schorer, *Sinclair Lewis: An American Life* (New York, 1961), pp. 153–54.

19. Quoted by Schorer, p. 466.

20. Quoted by Walker, p. 76.

21. Bierce to Sterling (n.d.), quoted by Walker, p. 102.

22. London to Sterling, November 16, 1910, *Letters from Jack*

London, ed. King Hendricks and Irving Shephard (New York, 1965), p. 321.

23. Sterling to Mary Austin, September 1, 1910; "Letters of George Sterling," p. 129.

24. Van Wyck Brooks, *An Autobiography* (New York, 1965), pp. 185–86.

25. Mary Craig Sinclair, *Southern Belle* (New York, 1957), p. 94.

26. Paul Fatout, *Ambrose Bierce: The Devil's Lexicographer* (Norman, Okla., 1951), p. 306.

27. *The Letters of Ambrose Bierce*, ed. Bertha Clark Pope (San Francisco, 1922), pp. 170–71.

28. Ibid., p. 308.

29. Ibid., pp. 196–97.

30. George Sterling, "The Shadow Maker," *American Mercury* 6 (September 1925): 18.

31. Ibid.

32. "The Passing of Bierce," *Sails and Mirage and Other Poems* (San Francisco, 1921), p. 60.

33. Sterling to John Myers O'Hara, December 20, 1913; "Letters of George Sterling," p. 268.

34. Edward O'Day, "1869–1926," *Overland Monthly* 85 (December 1927): 357.

35. Sterling to Albert Bender, October 22, 1914; "Letters of George Sterling," pp. 298–99.

36. Sterling to Jack London, September 12, 1907; "Letters of George Sterling," p. 99.

37. Harriet Monroe, "The Poetry of George Sterling," *Poetry* 8 (March 1916): 308–9.

38. Sterling to O'Hara, March 12, 1916; "Letters of George Sterling," p. 345.

39. Adela Rogers St. Johns, *Final Verdict* (Garden City, N.Y., 1962), p. 363.

40. O'Connor, pp. 395–96.

41. Ibid., p. 392.

42. Charmian London, "George Sterling," *Overland Monthly* 85 (March 1927): 70.

43. Sterling to Blanche Partington, December 10, 1916, Bancroft Library, University of California at Berkeley.

44. *The Binding of the Beast and Other War Verse* (San Francisco, 1917), p. 30.

45. Sterling to Blanche Partington, December 18, 1918, Bancroft Library, University of California at Berkeley.

46. Elsie Martinez interview, TS, Oral History Office, Library of University of California at Berkeley.

47. Sterling to Upton Sinclair, August 21, 1918; "Letters of George Sterling," p. 398.

48. "Spring in Carmel," *Selected Poems* (New York, 1923), p. 24.

49. Sterling to Charmian London, August 24, 1918; "Letters of George Sterling," pp. 399–400.

50. Idwal Jones, *Ark of Empire* (Garden City, N.Y., 1951), pp. 34–35.

51. Sterling to William Stanley Braithwaite, April 8, 1919; "Letters of George Sterling," p. 407.

52. Sterling to Walter Adolphe Roberts, February 7, 1920; "Letters of George Sterling," p. 423.

53. Mencken to Sterling, May 19, 1920, Huntington Library.

54. Sterling to Dreiser, February 10, 1920; "Letters of George Sterling," p. 424.

55. *Letters of Theodore Dreiser,* ed. Robert H. Elias (Philadelphia, 1959), I, 292–93.

56. Helen Dreiser, *My Life with Dreiser* (Cleveland, 1951), p. 53.

57. *Letters of Theodore Dreiser,* I, 292.

58. Ibid., I, 332.

59. "Introduction," *Lilith* (New York, 1926), p. xii.

60. George Sterling, *Robinson Jeffers: The Man and the Artist* (New York, 1926), p. 12.

61. Letter from Joan London to D.H. Gross, October 12, 1965, quoted by Gross, "Letters of George Sterling," p. 32.

62. Upton Sinclair, *My Lifetime in Letters* (Columbia, Mo., 1960), p. 250.

63. Miriam Allen DeFord, *They Were San Franciscans* (Caldwell, Idaho, 1941), p. 317.

64. Robert O'Brien, *This Is San Francisco* (New York, 1948), pp. 133–34.

65. Malcolm Cowley, *Exile's Return* (New York, 1969), p. 284.

66. Ibid., p. 247.

Chapter Three

1. Walter E Houghton and G. Robert Strange, eds., *Victorian Poetry and Poetics* (Boston, 1968), p. xviii.

2. William Charvat, "Literature as Business," in Robert Spiller et al., eds., *Literary History of the United States* (New York, 1948), II, 956.

3. Larzer Ziff, *The American 1890s* (New York, 1966), p. 123.

4. "Introduction,' *An American Anthology,* ed Edmund Clarence Stedman (New York, 1968), n.p.

5. Quoted by Ziff, p. 306.

6. Stedman, p. 560.

7. Ibid., p. 725.

8. Carlin T. Kindilien, *American Poetry in the Eighteen Nineties* (Providence, R.I., 1956), p. 12.

9. *The Collected Poems of Edwin Arlington Robinson* (New York, 1937). p. 93.

10. Kindilien, p. 11.

11. Joseph Lewis French, quoted by Richard O'Connor in *Ambrose Bierce: A Biography* (Boston, 1967), p. 190.

12. Quoted by O'Connor, *Ambrose Bierce,* p. 194.

13. Ibid., p. 208.

14. "The Shadow Maker," *American Mercury* 6 (September 1925): 11.

15. *The Collected Works of Ambrose Bierce* (New York, 1966), X, 143.

16. Ibid., X. 146.

17. Ibid., X, 148.

18. Ibid., XI, 175.

19. Ibid., XI, 176.

20. Ibid., XI, 183.

21. Ibid., X, 59.

22. Ibid., X, 274.

23. Ibid., X, 250.

24. Ibid., X, 254.

25. Ibid., XI, 180.

26. Quoted by O'Connor, p. 201.

27. *The Letters of Ambrose Bierce,* p. 40.

28. Ibid., p. 44.

29. Michael Orth, "A Biography of George Sterling." M.A. Thesis, San Francisco State College, 1963, p. 65.

30. Ibid., p 64.

31. Joseph Noel, *Footloose in Arcadia,* p. 72.

32. *Letters of Ambrose Bierce,* p. 53.

33. "Memorial Day, 1901," *The Testimony of the Suns and Other Poems* (San Francisco, 1903), p. 13. All subsequent references to poems by George Sterling in this chapter are from the same volume, and will be identified by page number references in parentheses in the text.

34. "Letters of George Sterling," p. 46.

35. *Letters of Ambrose Bierce*, p. 49.

36. "The Shadow Maker," p. 10.

37. *Letters of Ambrose Bierce*, p. 52.

38. Lionel Stevenson, "George Sterling's Place in Modern Poetry," *University of California Chronicle* 31 (October 1929): 416.

39. *Letters of Ambrose Bierce*, pp. 51–52.

40. Mark Schorer, *Sinclair Lewis*, p. 91.

41. Ernst Haekel, *The Riddle of the Universe* (New York, 1900), p. 248.

42. H. G. Wells, "Under the Knife," *The Short Stories of H. G. Wells* (London, 1960), pp. 414–15.

43. *Letters of Ambrose Bierce*, p. 55.

44. Stevenson, p. 418.

45. Margaret Marshall, "On Rereading Fitzgerald," *F. Scott Fitzgerald: The Man and His Work*, ed. Alfred Kazin (New York, 1951), p. 112.

46. *Testimony of the Suns*, p. 8.

47. Ambrose Bierce, *Collected Works*, X, 249.

Chapter Four

1. "Decadence," *Princeton Encyclopedia of Poetry and Poetics*, ed. Alex Preminger et al. (Princeton, N.J., 1974), p. 185.

2. *A Wine of Wizardry and Other Poems* (San Francisco, 1909), pp. 14–15. Subsequent references to the poem will be from this edition; they will be identified by page number references in the text.

3. *The Testimony of the Suns and Other Poems*, p. 84.

4. *A Wine of Wizardry and Oher Poems*, p. 20.

5. All references to poems in this section, identified by page number citations in the text, are drawn from *A Wine of Wizardry and Other Poems* (San Francisco, 1909).

6. Edward Engelberg, *The Symbolist Poem* (New York, 1967), p. 39.

7. "Three Sonnets of Oblivion," *Selected Poems* (New York, 1923), p. 145 Subsequent references to these three sonnets, iden tified by page numbers in the text, will be from this volume.

8. Alfred Kreymborg, *Our Singing Strength* (New York, 1929), p. 283.

9. *The House of Orchids and Other Poems* (San Francisco, 1911). Subsequent references to sonnets from this collection will be identified by page number citations in the text.

10. *Nation* 93 (October 26, 1911): 395.

11. *Saturday Review of Literature* 4 (June 23, 1928): 994.

12. *Sonnets to Craig* (New York, 1928), p. 47.

13. Lewis G Sterner, *The Sonnet in American Literature* (Philadelphia, 1930), p. 77.

14. All references to poems in this section, identified by page number citations in the text, are taken from *The House of Orchids and Other Poems*.

15. *New York Times,* June 25, 1911, p. 400.

16. Henry May, *The End of American Innocence* (Chicago, 1964), p. 88

Chapter Five

1. George Cabot Lodge, letter to Langdon Mitchell, quoted by Henry Adams in *The Life of George Cabot Lodge* (New York, 1911), p. 190.

2. "Ode on the Centenary of the Birth of Robert Browning," *Selected Poems* (New York, 1923), pp. 166–67. Subsequent references to the ode, identified by page numbers in the text, will be from this edition.

3. *Beyond the Breakers and Other Poems* (San Francisco, 1914), p. 24.

4. Edward F. O'Day, "Varied Types," *Town Talk* 20 (September 7, 1912): 7.

5. *Beyond the Breakers,* p. 23. Subsequent references to poems from this collection will be identified by page number citations in the text.

6. "Letters of George Sterling," p. 202.

7. Monroe, "The Poetry of George Sterling," p. 308.

8. *The Caged Eagle and Other Poems* (San Francisco, 1916), p. 20.

9. Ibid., p 21.

10. *Beyond the Breakers,* p. 74.

11. *A Wine of Wizardry and Other Poems,* pp. 60–61.

12. *Yosemite: An Ode* (San Francisco, 1915), p. 16.

13. "Letters of George Sterling," p. 505.

14. *Beyond the Breakers,* p. 45.

15. Ibid., p. 47.

16. *The Binding of the Beast and Other War Verse* (San Francisco, 1917), p. 21.

17. Ibid., p. 28.

18. Ibid., p. 15.
19. *The House of Orchids*, p. 23.
20. *The Binding of the Beast*, p. 44.
21. *Nation* 106 (June 29, 1918): 760.
22. Quoted in William Jay Smith, *The Spectra Hoax* (Middletown, Conn., 1961), p. 25.
23. "Rhymes and Reactions," *Overland Monthly* 85 (March 1927): 95.
24. *Sails and Mirage and Other Poems* (San Francisco, 1921), p. 21. Subsequent references to poems from this collection will be identified by page numbers in the text.
25. Arthur Symons, "The Decadent Movement in Literature," in *Victorian Poetry and Poetics*, p. 906.

Chapter Six

1. Neihardt's letters to Sterling are in the Sterling Collection, Huntington Library.
2. *Lilith: A Dramatic Poem* (New York, 1926), p. 75. Subsequent references to *Lilith*, indentified by page numbers in the text, will be from this edition.
3. "Letters of George Sterling," p. 538.
4. Ibid.
5. Ibid.
6. The essay has been printed in *Resources for American Literary Studies* 3 (1973): 230–48, with an introduction by Joseph W. Slade. I quote from the manuscript copy in the Bancroft Library.
7. "Letters of George Sterling," p. 491.
8. "The Shadow Maker," p. 10.
9. *Overland Monthly* 85 (March 1927): 95.
10. *After Sunset* (San Francisco, 1939), p. 28.
11. *Truth* (San Francisco, 1926), p. v. Except for one (note 12), the quotations from *Truth* in the following discussion are from the earlier and fuller edition (Chicago, 1923), and are identified by page numbers in the text.
12. *Truth* (San Francisco, 1926), pp. 43–4.

Chapter Seven

1. Kremborg, p. 285.
2. *A History of American Poetry: 1900–1940* (New York, 1946), p. 58.
3. *Arizona Quarterly* 13 (Spring 1957): 55.

4. (New York, 1959), p. 121.

5. *University of California Chronicle* 31 (October 1929): 407.

6. Ibid., p. 419.

7. *The Stone Mason of Tor House* (n.p., 1966), p. 145.

8. *The Selected Letters of Robinson Jeffers, 1897–1962*, ed. Ann Ridgeway (Baltimore, 1968), p. 26.

9. *The Critical Reputation of Robinson Jeffers: A Bibliographic Study* (Camden, Conn., 1974), pp. 5–6.

10. *The Selected Poetry of Robinson Jeffers* (New York, 1959), p. 365.

11. *Selected Letters*, p. 27.

12. Foreword to *Selected Poetry*, p. xiv.

Selected Bibliography

PRIMARY SOURCES

1. Published Titles (in chronological order)

The Testimony of the Suns and Other Poems. San Francisco: W. E. Wood, 1903.

The Triumph of Bohemia. San Francisco: The Bohemian Club, 1907.

A Wine of Wizardry and Other Poems. San Francisco: Robertson, 1909.

The House of Orchids and Other Poems. San Francisco: Robertson, 1911.

Beyond the Breakers and Other Poems. San Francisco: Robertson, 1914.

Ode on the Opening of the Panama and Pacific International Exposition. San Francisco: Robertson, 1915.

Yosemite: An Ode. San Francisco: Robertson, 1915.

The Evanescent City. San Francisco: Robertson, 1915.

The Caged Eagle and Other Poems. San Francisco: Robertson, 1916.

The Binding of the Beast and Other War Verse. San Francisco: Robertson, 1917.

Rosamund: A Dramatic Poem. San Francisco: Robertson, 1920.

Sails and Mirage and Other Poems. San Francisco: Robertson, 1921.

Selected Poems. New York: Holt, 1923.

Truth. Chicago: The Bookfellows, 1923.

Truth. San Francisco: The Bohemian Club, 1926.

Lilith: A Dramatic Poem. New York: Macmillan, 1926.

Robinson Jeffers: the Man and the Artist. New York: Boni and Liveright, 1926.

Sonnets to Craig. New York: A. and C. Boni, 1928.

Poems to Vera. New York: Oxford University Press, 1938.

After Sunset. San Francisco: Howell, 1939.

2. Memoirs

"The Shadow Maker," *American Mercury* 6 (September 1925): 10–19.

"Joaquin Miller," *American Mercury* 7 (February 1926): 220–29.
"A First-Class Fighting Man," *American Mercury* 10 (January 1927):
    76–80.

3. Letters.

Sterling was a prolific letter-writer, and his correspondence with
various literary figures is of great biographical and historical value.
Many of his letters have been collected by Dalton Harvey Gross, in
"The Letters of George Sterling," a 1968 doctoral dissertation at
Southern Illinois University. Below are other published collections
of letters by George Sterling.

DUKE, MAURICE. "Letters of George Sterling to James Branch Cabell,"
    American Literature 64 (1972): 146–53.

DUNBAR, JOHN R. "Letters of George Sterling to Carey McWilliams,"
    California Historical Society Quarterly 66 (1967): 235–52.

GROSS, DALTON H. "George Sterling's Letters to Theodore Dreiser:
    1920–1926," *Dreiser Newsletter* 4 (1973): 14–20.

————. "George Sterling's Life at Carmel: Sterling's Letters to
    Witter Bynner," *Markham Review* 4 (1973): 12–16.

————. "Seventeen George Sterling Letters," *Jack London News-
    letter* 1 (1968): 41–61.

HENRY, JAMES. "Give a Man a Boat He Can Sail," *Jack London News-
    letter* 7 (1974): 23–29.

1. Biography

There is as yet no published biography of George Sterling. Insights
into his relationships with other writers may be derived from exam-
ining the biographies and letters of Ambrose Bierce, Jack London,
Upton Sinclair, Sinclair Lewis, H. L. Mencken, Theodore Dreiser,
and Robinson Jeffers. Valuable reminiscences about Sterling may be
found in the memorial editions of *Overland Monthly*—March, November, and December 1927. The following are also important
sources of biographical information.

AUSTIN, MARY. "George Sterling at Carmel." *American Mercury* 11
    (May 1927): 65–72.

BENEDIKTSSON, THOMAS. "The Life of George Sterling." Doctoral
    dissertation, University of Washington, 1974.

BENNET, RAINE E. "Don Passé." *Literary Review* 15 (1972): 133–47.

DEFORD, MIRIAM ALLEN. *They Were San Franciscans.* Caldwell, Idaho: Caxton Printers, 1941.

DITZLER, ROBERT. "Bohemianism in San Francisco at the Turn of the Century." M.A. Thesis, University of Washington, 1966.

FLEMING, DONALD. "The Last Bohemian." *Quarterly News-Letter* [Book Club of California], 37 (1972): 75–95.

NOEL, JOSEPH. *Footloose in Arcadia: A Personal Record of Jack London, George Sterling and Ambrose Bierce.* New York: Carrick and Evans, 1940.

ORTH, MICHAEL. "A Biography of George Sterling." M.A. Thesis, San Francisco State College, 1963.

PARRY, ALBERT. *Garrets and Pretenders.* New York: Covici, Friede, 1933.

WALKER, FRANKLIN. *The Seacoast of Bohemia: An Account of Early Carmel.* San Francisco: Book Club of California, 1966.

2. Criticism.

Sterling's poems have never received extended critical attention. The following are representative viewpoints, arranged chronologically.

BIERCE, AMBROSE. "A Poet and His Poem." *Cosmopolitan* 43 (September 1907): 575–77. The first review of Sterling's work to appear in a major periodical. Written to accompany the publication of "A Wine of Wizardry" in the same issue of the magazine, the article praises Sterling as "a very great poet—incomparably the greatest that we have on this side of the Atlantic."

————. "An Insurrection of the Peasantry." *Cosmopolitan* 44 (December 1907): 222–26. A rebuttal of the negative criticisms of "A Wine of Wizardry," broadly ironic in tone.

MONROE, HARRIET. "The Poetry of George Sterling." *Poetry* 8 (March 1916): 307–308. A representative Imagist viewpoint, praising Sterling's lyric gift but condemning his use of Tennysonian rhetoric.

KREYMBORG, ALFRED. *Our Singing Strength.* New York: Coward-McCann, 1929. Contains an assessment of Sterling's work which apparently is based upon the most frequently anthologized poems. Criticizes the tendency toward allusion and archaism as "a tragic epitome of the adventure of many American poets among books and bookishness," but expresses admiration for the sonnets.

STEVENSON, LIONEL. "George Sterling's Place in Modern Poetry." *University of California Chronicle* 31 (October 1929): 401–21. The best critical exploration of Sterling's poems. Asserts that Sterling is nearly the only American poet of his generation who attached himself to the English literary tradition. Discusses in detail the interplay of devotion to beauty and fatalism in Sterling's work.

GREGORY, HORACE, and ZATURENSKA, MAURYA. *A History of American Poetry, 1900–1940.* New York: Harcourt, Brace, 1942. Discusses Sterling as a transitional poet of the "twilight interval" before the Imagist rebellion. Notes the "persistent note of pathos as well as a fitfully expressed sense of evil" which underlie Sterling's work.

COBLENTZ, STANTON. "George Sterling: Western Phenomenon." *Arizona Quarterly* 13 (Spring 1957): 54–60. A laudatory discussion of Sterling's poetry by a critic whose abiding allegiances are with the nineteenth century.

ANGOFF, CHARLES. *George Sterling: A Centenary Memoir-Anthology.* New York: A. S. Barnes, 1969. Another sympathetic introduction to Sterling's work by a conservative critic.

Index

177